The Complete Guide to Eco-Friendly House Cleaning:

Everything You Need to Know Explained Simply

By Anne Kocsis

THE COMPLETE GUIDE TO ECO-FRIENDLY HOUSE CLEANING: EVERYTHING YOU NEED TO KNOW EXPLAINED SIMPLY

Library of Congress Cataloging-in-Publication Data

Kocsis, Anne B., 1965-
  The complete guide to eco-friendly house cleaning : everything you need to know explained simply / by Anne B. Kocsis.
      p. cm.
  Includes bibliographical references and index.
  ISBN-13: 978-1-60138-366-2 (alk. paper)
  ISBN-10: 1-60138-366-5 (alk. paper)
  1. House cleaning. 2. Household supplies. 3. Green products. I. Title.
  TX324.K63 2009
  648--dc22
                        2009045278

Printed in the United States

PROJECT MANAGER: Kimberly Fulscher • kfulscher@atlantic-pub.com
PEER REVIEWER: Marilee Griffin • mgriffin@atlantic-pub.com
INTERIOR DESIGN: Samantha Martin • smartin@atlantic-pub.com
ASSISTANT EDITOR: Angela Pham • apham@atlantic-pub.com
FRONT & BACK COVER DESIGNER: Jackie Miller • millerjackiej@gmail.com

Printed on Recycled Paper

We recently lost our beloved pet "Bear," who was not only our best and dearest friend but also the "Vice President of Sunshine" here at Atlantic Publishing. He did not receive a salary but worked tirelessly 24 hours a day to please his parents. Bear was a rescue dog that turned around and showered myself, my wife, Sherri, his grandparents Jean, Bob, and Nancy, and every person and animal he met (maybe not rabbits) with friendship and love. He made a lot of people smile every day.

We wanted you to know that a portion of the profits of this book will be donated to The Humane Society of the United States. *—Douglas & Sherri Brown*

The human-animal bond is as old as human history. We cherish our animal companions for their unconditional affection and acceptance. We feel a thrill when we glimpse wild creatures in their natural habitat or in our own backyard.

Unfortunately, the human-animal bond has at times been weakened. Humans have exploited some animal species to the point of extinction.

The Humane Society of the United States makes a difference in the lives of animals here at home and worldwide. The HSUS is dedicated to creating a world where our relationship with animals is guided by compassion. We seek a truly humane society in which animals are respected for their intrinsic value, and where the human-animal bond is strong.

Want to help animals? We have plenty of suggestions. Adopt a pet from a local shelter, join The Humane Society and be a part of our work to help companion animals and wildlife. You will be funding our educational, legislative, investigative and outreach projects in the U.S. and across the globe.

Or perhaps you'd like to make a memorial donation in honor of a pet, friend or relative? You can through our Kindred Spirits program. And if you'd like to contribute in a more structured way, our Planned Giving Office has suggestions about estate planning, annuities, and even gifts of stock that avoid capital gains taxes.

Maybe you have land that you would like to preserve as a lasting habitat for wildlife. Our Wildlife Land Trust can help you. Perhaps the land you want to share is a backyard—that's enough. Our Urban Wildlife Sanctuary Program will show you how to create a habitat for your wild neighbors.

So you see, it's easy to help animals. And The HSUS is here to help.

THE HUMANE SOCIETY
OF THE UNITED STATES.

2100 L Street NW • Washington, DC 20037 • 202-452-1100
www.hsus.org

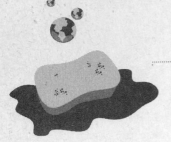

Trademarks

All trademarks, trade names, or logos mentioned or used are the property of their respective owners and are used only to directly describe the products being provided. Every effort has been made to properly capitalize, punctuate, identify, and attribute trademarks and trade names to their respective owners, including the use of ® and ™ wherever possible and practical. Atlantic Publishing Group, Inc. is not a partner, affiliate, or licensee with the holders of said trademarks.

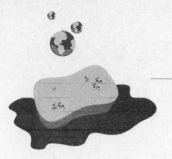

Disclaimer

The Green Seal name and logo is a trademark and property of the Green Seal Corporation.

The Design for the Environment name and logo is a trademark and property of United States Environmental Protection Agency.

The Safer Detergents Stewardship Initiative name and logo is a trademark and property of United States Environmental Protection Agency.

The Tender Corporation name and logo is a trademark and property of Tender Corporation.

The Dyna-E International name and logo is a trademark and property of Dyna-E International.

The Seventh Generation name and logo is a trademark and property of Seventh Generation, Inc.

The Simple Green name and logo is a trademark and property of Sunshine Makers, Inc.

The Nature's Source name and logo is a trademark and property of S.C. Johnson & Son, Inc.

The Green Works name and logo is a trademark and property of The Clorox Company.

The Method name and logo is a registered trademark and property of Method Products, Inc.

The Mrs. Meyer's Clean Day name and logo is a trademark and property of the Caldrea Company Corporation.

The Shaklee name and logo is a trademark and property of the Shaklee Corporation.

The Oxi Clean name and logo is a trademark and property of Orange Glo International, Inc.

The Wash-it Laundry Ball name and logo is a trademark and property of Shenzen Become Industry and Trade Co., Ltd.

The Static Eliminator name and logo is a trademark and property of Maddocks Engineering Ltd. Corporation.

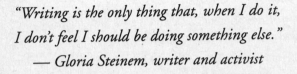

Dedication

"*Writing is the only thing that, when I do it,*
I don't feel I should be doing something else."
— *Gloria Steinem, writer and activist*

I wish to dedicate this book to my family and friends for their love and support during the difficult times. I also wish to thank them for their enthusiastic desire to embrace this project. Their questions and experiences made me delve deeper and hopefully make this a better book. In particular, I wish to thank my children: John, for his willingness to double-check my facts; and Matt and Katie, whose love of science made them avid research assistants. Thank you all for believing in me.

Table of Contents

Chapter 2: The First Step · 47

Chapter 3: What are the Options? · 57

Chapter 4: New, Greener Products Hit the Market   81

Chapter 5: Clean, Green Science   93

Chapter 6: Where to Start   109

Chapter 7: Working From Top to Bottom   127

Chapter 8: Confronting the Kitchen   151

Chapter 9: Battling the Bathroom   183

Chapter 10: Liberating the Laundry Room 207

Chapter 11: Wrestling With the Rest of the House   227

Chapter 12: Eco-Friendly Pet Care   **245**

Chapter 13: Dealing With Dirt Outdoors · 251

Chapter 14: Surface Cleaning Simplified · 265

Chapter 15: Conquering Specific Stains   275

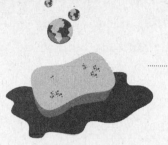

Foreword

Green Seal

We clean our homes to provide a safe place for our families to live and grow in. However, in our desire to create a safe haven, we often do more harm than good. Many conventional cleaners contain carcinogens, mutagens, and endocrine disruptors, not to mention volatile organic compounds, which can contribute to asthma and allergic reactions. When used, these cleaners are released into the air or down the drain, contributing to indoor air pollution and smog formation, which can negatively impact the environment with their high toxicity and phosphorus levels.

The good news is that over the last few years, we have seen a proliferation of green cleaning products that offer effective cleaning without sacrificing the health of the environment or our families. But while some of these are indeed safer alternatives to the harsh cleaners we have relied on in the past, others are little more than toxic cleaners disguised in bottles covered with leaves and flowers. In her new book *The Complete Guide to Eco-Friendly House Cleaning: Everything You Need to Know Explained Simply*, Anne B. Kocsis helps us navigate the tricky waters of green cleaning. She also provides many handy homemade cleaning solutions that are easy on the wallet.

A true green cleaning program goes beyond the cleaning solutions used and includes the equipment and procedures, too. Kocsis identifies everything you need to get started in this straightforward guide to cleaning your home — with your family, your pets, and the environment in mind.

Charlotte Peyraud
Marketing & Outreach Associate

Green Seal Inc: An independent, non-profit organization that provides science-based environmental certification standards for green products.

www.greenseal.org

Author's Note

"*Housework, if you do it right, will kill you.*"

— Erma Bombeck, author and humorist

American humorist Erma Bombeck was joking when she made that statement. But, sadly, given the way housecleaning has evolved over the last century, it is not too far removed from the truth. We continue to disinfect our homes in order to kill any potential germ that could possibly make us sick. Ironically, we have actually made ourselves sicker in the process because of the chemicals we are using. Hopefully, as we have completed the first decade of the 21st century, we are more aware of the dangers involved in using unnecessary chemicals in our homes. As researchers make information available, we are forced to rethink the way we maintain our homes. Most of us use products we do not really need. As we start to simplify our lives, we realize that some of the things our ancestors did more than 100 years ago actually made sense.

Granted, I am not a purist by any stretch of the imagination — I personally would be lost without indoor plumbing. However, I do believe we can simplify our lives and improve conditions for our families and the environment just by making a few uncomplicated changes in the way we perform simple household chores. In this book, I have compiled information about homemade cleaning products that are more eco-friendly, healthier to use, and less expensive than many store-bought products.

I am an average representative of soccer moms everywhere who are faced with concerns for their family's health, as well as the family budget. The housecleaning changes I have made over the last ten years have come from necessity and imagination. There are many good reasons to make your lifestyle more environmentally friendly, and I will address many of them. I am here to help you make some positive changes in the simplest way possible for you and your family. If it is not simple, most of us will not do it, and if we do, we will not stick to it for very long. So like all other journeys, this one starts with a single step. Approach it with a good attitude and a sense of humor, and you will be fine.

Over the years, my children, my husband, and I have suffered numerous ailments. Many were minor colds, viruses, and rashes; others were more serious. One of my sons suffers from debilitating headaches; the other one has asthma and allergies. My daughter has endured joint pain issues and some minor skin conditions. My son Matt often jokes about our house being built on ancient burial grounds and causing us bad luck in the health department.

I joked about it with my friends, yet I found myself doing whatever I could to try to get rid of germs in the house. I repeatedly washed linens and scrubbed walls and floors. We hired a pest control company and had industrial companies clean our carpets. We paid to have our ducts cleaned and sprayed to remove mold and mildew. Despite spending a lot of time, energy, and money trying to improve conditions for my family, things did not get better.

Through it all, my friends would listen to me lament about the latest illness. We would joke about the unlikelihood of one family having to deal with so many medical problems in such short periods of time. I often said I would write a book about it someday. The plan was to write a humorous account of all the health escapades we endured. Instead, the opportunity arose to write a more important book: one that tells how to prevent some of them from happening in the first place.

As a freelance writer and stay-at-home mother, I researched ways to do things around the house that could save money. During this research, I came across information about homemade cleaning products and the fact that they were not only less expensive, but also much healthier. As I changed the way I do things in my own home, I was rewarded with a significant improvement in the overall health of my family. We no longer have to deal with asthma, and we have substantially fewer colds, headaches, and other ailments. Throughout this book, I share the information I discovered in my research. It includes information on the cleaning product industry, government regulations, and simple solutions to numerous household-cleaning situations.

Introduction

In many ways, our society continues to progress in ways most of us would not part with. At times, however, improvements cause problems. For example, Thalidomide was considered a wonder drug upon its creation in the 1940s. It was given to pregnant women in the 1950s and 1960s to combat morning sickness. Unfortunately, it was later found to cause devastating birth defects and became a banned substance. Now, more than a half a century later, researchers are reviewing what went wrong in an attempt to reformulate the drug for other uses.

The same situation occurs today in the cleaning product industry. As the United States developed into an industrialized nature, individuals noticed the effects of the country's growth on the environment. Thus, an environmental movement slowly emerged. As manufacturers created new products, environmentalists urged the government to enact new laws and regulations to deal with the repercussions from using the products. In respect to the cleaning product industry, companies marketed stronger cleaning products to combat bacterial germs and increasing illness. Unfortunately, as a side effect, certain ailments like asthma, allergies, and upper respiratory illnesses became more prevalent.

In addition to airborne pollutants causing harm to humans, many of these cleaning products entered soil and water systems, creating problems with the ecosystem. The damage has had a domino effect: Plants and animals are affected, thereby affecting food and water supplies. The government and many independent agencies continue to do research to improve the issue. As a result, many companies are revamping their formulas to create products that, when used properly, will have less of a negative impact on consumers. However, this does not mean the problem has been solved. There are still long-term effects from damage that has already occurred. People have products in their homes that are old and potentially hazardous, and many possibly dangerous chemicals still exist in, and on, commonly used products and furnishings.

As recently as May 2009, the United Nations Environment Program banned nine chemicals. Research is ongoing, but it takes a long time to gather enough evidence to prove that a substance should require caution and regulation. Therefore, this book is designed to serve two primary functions. It will help you:

- Identify potentially dangerous substances you may currently be using in your home.

- Assist you in finding suitable alternative solutions.

To comprehend both, it is helpful to understand how we got where we are today.

History of the Environmental Movement

Concern for the environment is currently a hot topic of discussion, but it is not a new topic. The environmental movement in this country actually goes back to the early part of the 1800s. One of the earliest known American proponents of the movement was Henry David Thoreau, author of *Walden; or, Life in the Woods*, published in 1854. Another American famous for his efforts in this area is John Muir. He was a naturalist who founded the Sierra Club in 1892. Regardless of these individuals' efforts and many like them, it was almost 75 years later that the United States started considering the damage being done to the environment and the people who inhabit it.

American society started to pay more attention to the issue in the early 1960s. In 1962, an American marine biologist named Rachel Carson wrote a book titled *Silent Spring*, outlining the damaging effects of pesticide to the environment. Specifically, it exposed the hazards of using the chemical DDT, a substance that is now banned.

During the 1970s, the U.S. government made attempts to address the public's concerns. In 1970, the U.S. government formed the Environmental Protection Agency (EPA) to work with and educate the public, and Congress signed the Clean Air Act. In 1972, the United Nations established a worldwide environmental committee, and Congress signed amendments to the Federal Water Pollution Control Act. The amendments, known as the Clean Water Act (CWA), specified regulations for toxic substances that affect the water supply. A few years later, in 1978, President Jimmy Carter declared a state of public health emergency over a situation in Love Canal, New York.

William T. Love had purchased three blocks of land, which became Love Canal near Niagara Falls. His vision was to power the homes and industry nearby from the rivers and falls with the use of the small canal in the early 1900s. The experiment failed and, in the 1920s, the land became a municipal and industrial chemical waste-dumping site. In 1953, the Hooker Chemical Company filled in the dump with dirt and sold it to the city for $1. Twenty-five years later, a record amount of rainfall triggered an explosion of leaching that unearthed the waste. The eruption caused chemicals to invade the school and people's homes. It even uprooted a swimming pool. The chemicals caused multiple birth defects and cases of cancer in the townspeople. More than 200 families had to be evacuated.

At the time, President Carter called the Love Canal situation "one of the grimmest discoveries of the modern era." Since then, many government agencies and subcommittees have worked to prevent this from happening again. It is now more than 30 years later, and many changes have occurred worldwide. It is important to note that the dumping took place in the 1920s, but the deadly consequences transpired more than 50 years later. The accumulation of chemicals over time can cause more significant problems; therefore, we cannot always assume that what we do presently does not matter.

Considering research over time, one particular committee has already banned multiple substances worldwide: the United Nations Environment Programme (UNEP). Governments worldwide designated task forces to evaluate the effects of chemical substances. During the early part of the 21st century, 21 substances were banned from use — manufacturers were prohibited from using them in the production of regular household substances. The ban does, however, allow certain parts of the chemicals to be used in specific circumstances. For example, the chemical chlordane was previously used on corn and citrus crops, and in common lawn fertilizers in our country. Once it was added to the list of banned substances, manufacturers were restricted to using it in certain items, such as termiticide products and plywood adhesives. Indeed, the products have been banned, but they are not all completely forbidden. Even the chemicals that have no exemptions, such as Endrin, can still linger in the air, water, and soil. *Learn about these substances in more detail in Chapter 1.* Today, the UNEP continues to evaluate toxic substances around the world. According to their Web site, they have a committee dedicated to assisting countries with product waste that causes harm to human health and the environment. That includes the following:

- Persistent, bio-accumulative and toxic substances (PBTs)
- Chemicals that are carcinogens or mutagens, or that adversely affect the reproductive, endocrine, immune, or nervous systems
- Chemicals that have immediate hazards (acutely toxic, explosives, corrosives)
- Chemicals of global concern such as persistent organic pollutants (POPs), greenhouse gases, and ozone-depleting substances (ODS)
- Health care wastes
- Electronic equipment disposal, commonly known as e-wastes

Many of the toxic substances that existed in the later part of the 20th century have been banned from use in new products. The problem is that some of these substances still exist in multiple forms. They might dwell as ingredients in older products sitting around your home, as protective coating on clothing and furnishings, or in landfills not far from where you live. For that reason, this book explains the multiple dangers that exist from exposure to toxic chemicals, as well as provides simple, non-toxic alternatives to cleaning your home.

As a result of growing public awareness and government involvement, scientists began studying the effects of the chemicals in commonly used products such as fertilizer, pest control, cleaning products, and personal grooming items. The studies revealed detrimental side effects created by many advanced products. The chemicals used to make improvements, such as to increase a product's usability and shelf life, actually created problems for human health and the ecosystem. Now, companies must re-evaluate their past, present, and future methods of creating, using, and disposing of common household products.

The growing amount of information resulted in a new branch of scientific research, known as environmental science, whereby scientists review the affects of our lifestyle on the environment. Subsequently, another new field called "environmental medicine" emerged. It incorporates environmental science, chemistry, and medicine. In this area, the toxicity of chemical substances on humans is researched and studied. It is through these areas of scientific research that we now have more public information on the harmful health effects caused by toxic substances commonly used in the average consumer household.

How Does This Relate to Me?

Over the past few decades, the U.S. government created more agencies and task forces to manage the increasing environmental concerns. Additionally, U.S. agencies participate in environmental committees on the global front. Despite frequent news reports about the various task forces concerning environmental impact, many individuals still do not fully comprehend how these issues affect them in their daily lives.

Instead, people focus on more obvious issues that do affect them regularly. News reports depict food products recalled because of E. coli, schools closing as a result of swine flu outbreaks, and antibiotics losing effectiveness with overuse. To compound the problem, people worry about job security and are fearful of staying home from work if they become ill. The end result is a nation of individuals who understandably become diligent in fighting bacteria any way they can.

Despite growing concerns about toxic chemicals and the environment, people remain focused on cleanliness and germ-killing products. As a result, companies introduced new merchandise in the 1990s and early 2000s that boasted claims of being antibacterial. Existing products were repackaged to include claims of having germ-fighting capabilities. People started carrying antibacterial hand sanitizers at all times, and schools and hospitals provided antibacterial hand sanitizer dispensers at stations every 3 feet. The intention was to kill all the potentially threatening microorganisms making the news. Unfortunately, the solution created another problem.

What Does "Antibacterial" Mean?

A product is termed "antibacterial" when agents are added to it for the express purpose of killing bacteria. The common additives are alcohol and Triclosan. Triclosan is produced from oxidizing the chemical benzene. But recent research now shows that these additives do not necessarily kill germs any more effectively than regular soap and warm water, and the use of these products is a source of great debate. There is some concern that the overuse of these products is creating strains of bacteria resistant to cleaning agents, in the same manner that the overuse of antibiotics have led to strains of bacteria that are resistant to medicines. Additionally, research performed at the Virginia Polytechnic Institute and State University indicated that products containing Triclosan form the carcinogenic substance chloroform when combined with chlorinated tap water. The EPA is currently tracking the university's research.

Since 2000, the American Medical Association (AMA) advised the Food and Drug Administration (FDA) to monitor the use of antibacterial products and their effects. Antibacterial additives are the most current source of debate among chemical-based products. But there are many other chemicals in products you use around the house every day that are not good for your family or the environment.

What Can We Do?

The EPA and the Consumer Product Safety Commission (CPSC) recently released a report titled *The Inside Story: A Guide to Indoor Air Quality*. The report states that because most people spend close to 90 percent of their time indoors, indoor air pollution is causing greater health risks than exterior air pollution. It suggests that everything — from heating and cooling to furnishings and cleaning products — affect the quality of the air we breathe in our own homes. Specifically, the report states that many dangerous pollutants are two to five times greater indoors than out.

Thus, the environmental movement has progressed beyond concern over pesticides and growing landfills; it is literally hitting home. The need for more eco-friendly products affects all aspects of everyday life, as the products consumers use daily in grooming and cleaning can create serious health risks. Normal usage, misusage, accidental ingestion, spilling, storage, and disposal can all cause damage, and companies are attempting to manufacture products that are less toxic, have more detailed warning labels, and will not hurt the environment upon disposal. As more information becomes available, they continue to research materials and potential health risks to users, while developing new formulas and labeling for their products.

Many companies are trying to become "green," but consumers still need to be aware of potential dangers. Knowledge is the key. Consumers need to learn how to read labels and understand risks. First, check the labels of any products that have sat around the house for more than a year. This is critical given the changes in regulations and the number of substances that have been banned during the last decade. Awareness of the current market is also crucial, as products change every day. Multiple products are being labeled "green," but what does that mean, exactly? In many cases, it may only mean that more water has been added to a previous formula to make it less caustic. This book provides information on the regulations that exist today and the safest alternatives for your family.

What Does "Green" Mean?

When people discuss the environment and anything that relates to its preservation, they use the word "green." It is used to describe people, politicians, and even products. In fact, the latest edition of the Merriam-Webster Dictionary has added this to the list of definitions for the word green: "tending to preserve environmental quality, such as being recyclable, biodegradable, or nonpolluting." Given that definition, the terms "green," "environmentally safe," and "eco-friendly" are used synonymously throughout this book.

"Eco-friendly" specifically means ecologically friendly; in other words, the item in question will not damage any part of the ecosystem. Eco-friendly items are biodegradable and do not contain hazardous chemicals. The concept of eco-friendly housecleaning as it applies here concerns all aspects of surface cleaning, caretaking, and maintenance. This book, therefore, addresses cleaning, organizing, using eco-friendly products and materials, yard maintenance, water usage, pest control, trash, and recycling. Americans enjoy convenience, but if you are willing to sacrifice a few minor conveniences, you can reduce the number of potential risks. Take the time to research the products you have around the house, and consider making some of your own. When you are done with household products, look into correct methods for disposal and recycling. Along those lines, the containers may be potentially toxic as well. If containers carrying toxic substances end up in the landfill, they can create lingering hazards. The landfill may not be near your home, but it can still affect your health when items stationed in it poison the surrounding soil and water. Scientists continue to provide information on the detrimental effects of many products. Subsequently, manufacturers are starting to label all kinds of products as "eco-friendly." The list includes just about everything. The words "non-toxic," "biodegradable," and "green" show up on many types of labels for food, clothing, furniture, fuels, appliances, and cleaning products. There are now so many products listed as green that it is hard to discern what is actually a viable, eco-friendly alternative versus what is just a marketing ploy. This book is intended to help sort out the information to help you make positive choices in your home that are good for your family and the environment. It includes the following:

- Facts about the dangerous chemicals in most homes
- Tips on identifying dangerous products currently in your home
- Lists of many of the available alternatives
- Suggestions for easy changes to make right now
- Assistance in decoding the labels on the multitude of green products currently on the market
- Simple formulas for making your own products with common household ingredients
- A guide to room-by-room cleaning
- Eco-friendly suggestions for cleaning all types of surfaces
- Environmentally safe ways to remove stains without toxic stain removers
- Hints for trash and recycling

Chapter 1

Domestic Dangers in Disguise

"The important thing in science is not so much to obtain new facts as to discover new ways of thinking about them."

— Sir William Henry Bragg, British physicist

Persistent Organic Pollutants (POPs)

Eco-friendly products are becoming more prevalent, but that does not mean that toxic substances no longer exist. You may have products sitting in your home, yard, garage, or other storage area that could contain toxic ingredients. Additionally, you may own furnishings and electronics that were coated in toxic substances. Landfills not far from your home may be full of chemicals. Despite the fact that some very dangerous elements were banned from being used in new products, you may not be completely safe from them. People keep objects and products in their homes for years. An old can of paint, a sofa that has been in your family for years, or an aerosol spray can in your garage — they all have the potential to affect your health. For that reason, you need to be aware of the persistent organic pollutants (POPs).

The UNEP met at the Stockholm Convention in 2001 and declared several substances to be toxic enough to be banned worldwide. The products displayed carcinogenic and neurotoxin side effects; scientific evidence linked these substances to cancer and nervous system disorders in numerous humans and animals. The first 12 chemicals identified as harmful persistent organic pollutants (POPs) were named the "dirty dozen." One of the biggest problems with these substances is the fact that they are mostly insoluble in water.

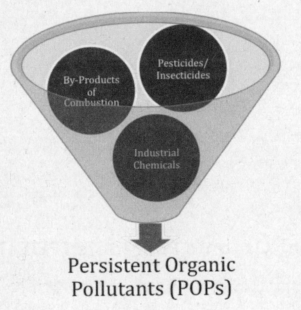

By-Products of Combustion

Pesticides/ Insecticides

Industrial Chemicals

Persistent Organic Pollutants (POPs)

The POPs can be divided into three basic categories: industrial chemicals, pesticides, and byproducts of the combustion process. They were found in plastics and a variety of common personal care and household cleaning products.

In May 2009, the UNEP added nine more substances to that original list of 12 products. Like the previous dozen, these substances accumulate in the tissue of all living things. The result over time is severe health consequences such as cancer, developmental issues, and reproductive problems.

These chemicals are predominantly found in flame-retardants used on furnishings, electronics, and clothing. The others are found in insecticides, like the products used in the treatment of lice and scabies. This group of dangerous chemicals was dubbed the "nasty nine."

The Dirty Dozen	The Nasty Nine
Aldrin	Pentabromodiphenyl ether
Chlordane	Octabromodiphenyl ether
DDT	Chlorodecone
Dieldrin	Lindane or hexachlorocyclohexane
Dioxin	Alpha-hexachlorocycloexane
Furans	Beta-hexachlorocyclohexane
Heptachlor	Perfluro otanesulponic acid or perfluoro octane sultonate (PFOs)
Hexachlorobenzene	Hexabromobiphenyl
Mirex	Pentachlorobenzene
Polychlorinated dioxins	
Polychlorinated furans	
Toxaphene	

Identifying Products Containing POPs

The original dirty dozen were identified in 2001. Since then, the products containing those chemicals have either been discontinued or heavily regulated. Products marketed today require detailed labeling. The problem is that many people have chemical-based products around their homes for long periods of time. This is particularly an issue with the nasty nine chemicals identified in May 2009. Many of these substances were used in flame-retardants and stain protection used on furnishings and electronics. It is also a problem with clothes that are kept for several years.

Additional information is available through a division of the U.S. Department of Health and Human Services. The division is a federal public health agency known as the Agency for Toxic Substances & Disease Registry (ATSDR). According to their Web site, the agency's goal is to help the public discern information and prevent adverse health conditions from harmful exposures related to toxic substances. The Web site includes a link called ToxFAQs™ that summarizes information regarding hazardous substances and potential exposure risks. To read these facts, visit **www.atsdr. cdc.gov/toxfaq.html** and search the substance in question.

Volatile Organic Compounds (VOCs)

In addition to being concerned with household items that may still contain POPs, you need to also be aware of other dangerously toxic byproducts that have not been banned. Some examples of these substances come in the form of volatile organic compounds (VOCs). VOCs are gases that emanate from other substances. They are emitted from many liquid and solid substances and pose a serious health risk to humans and animals when used in enclosed spaces with prolonged exposure. For that reason, the EPA states that some of these substances are up to ten times more likely to pose a health risk to people indoors.

These chemicals, often found in common household products, can irritate all the senses, create confusion and headaches, and can even cause long-term damage to internal organs, like the liver and kidneys. VOCs can evaporate readily and are not necessarily associated with an odor. People use thousands of these types of compounds in multitudes of products every day.

Some common examples of these compounds are benzene, ethylene glycol, formaldehyde, methylene chloride, perchloroethylene, toluene, xylene, and 1,3-butadiene. The compounds are found in numerous household products, such as aerosol sprays, air fresheners, disinfectants, spray cleaners, paints, paint strippers, and many solvents. The U.S. Department of Health and Human Services has a Web site to assist you in determining the potential risks posed by substances you currently have in your home, called the Household Products Database, which is maintained by the National Library of Medicine. The address is **http://hpd.nlm.nih.gov**.

The Web site includes a database listing of more than 8,000 consumer products that have harmful side effects to human and animal health. The brand names listed have been linked with the side effects from information gathered on the Material Safety Data Sheets (MSDS) provided by manufacturers. This information allows consumers to check products based on their ingredients. According the Web site, the database provides answers to the following questions:

- Which chemical ingredients are in which product brands? What percentage of these chemicals exists in these particular products?

- Who manufactures these brands, and how do I contact them with problems or concerns?

- Which chemical ingredients in which products produce harmful health effects? What are the acute and chronic effects of these chemicals?

- What other information is available about chemicals?

The risks concerning these chemicals are primarily dependent on the concentration of the substance in the enclosed area and how long an individual has been breathing it in. When researching volatile organic compounds, scientists study both short- and long-term health effects on the subject. The effects are broken into categories. Symptoms that appear within a few hours or a couple of days, and that are mild to moderately irritating, are considered to be a result of acute exposure. If symptoms are more severe and more pronounced for a prolonged long period of time, they are deemed to be the consequence of chronic exposure.

This is entirely different from individuals exposed to specific toxic substances in their work environment. Indoor air that contains just trace amount of these compounds over time can cause health issues. Here are examples of symptoms that may result from exposure to such compounds:

Acute Exposure Symptoms	Chronic Exposure Health Threats
Red, irritated eyes	Asthma
Headaches	Nervous system damage
Minor respiratory problems	Chronic respiratory problems
Dizziness	Cancer
Throat irritation	Liver damage
Confusion	Kidney damage
Allergies	
Vomiting	
Nausea	

Material Safety Data Sheet (MSDS)

◆MSDSonline®

With the constantly changing regulations, companies are required to prepare a document known as a material safety data sheet (MSDS). The MSDS provides information on chemicals used on a daily basis, rather than on an occasional basis. Therefore, an MSDS provides information on any potential harm or health side effect that each chemical could cause, as well as an emergency course of action.

The U.S. government's Occupational Safety and Health Administration (OSHA) began requiring MSDS documentation for all hazardous substances in May 1986. The documentation includes the correct use and handling, health risks and side effects, substance evaluations, storage recommendations, and what should take place in an emergency regarding the products.

MSDSs are used worldwide, but each country has its own laws regarding their usage. In the United States, there is a Hazard Communication Standard, which requires MSDS usage in any workplace where potentially hazardous substances are being handled. OSHA maintains these laws.

Although consumer products, including household chemicals, are not required to carry MSDSs at this point in time, the documentation is available online for many products. For more specific information, check the manufacturer's Web site.

CASE STUDY: UNDERSTANDING THE MATERIAL SAFETY DATA SHEET.

MSDSonline
350 N. Orleans St., Ste. 950
Chicago, IL 60654
1-888-362-2007
www.MSDSonline.com

MSDSonline makes products and provides services that protect environmental health around the world. They also access, manage, and display material safety data sheets (MSDS) and other vital safety information. Their database contains millions of original MSDS documents, and more than 10,000 new or amended MSDS documents are added to their database on a weekly basis.

The OSHA Hazard Communication Standard, also known as, 29 CFR 1910.1200, governs the communication of hazards associated with chemicals in the workplace.

The regulation was first adopted in the early 1980s and is a relatively straight-forward regulation. Although the regulation itself is dozens of pages long, the requirements can be summarized in four common-sense parts:

CASE STUDY: UNDERSTANDING THE MATERIAL SAFETY DATA SHEET.

1. **Written plan**
2. **Labels & warnings**
3. **Material safety data sheets**
4. **Training**

Written plan: Employers need a written plan for their Hazard Communication program. It should reflect the hazards their employees face each day and must include a current list of all hazardous chemicals. It must have a designated individual responsible for it, and the list needs to be easily accessible. The plan must also describe how each facility meets the requirements for labeling, MSDS management, and training.

Labels & warnings: According to the Hazard Communication regulation, all listed chemicals must be properly labeled. Additionally, the appropriate hazard warnings must be posted in the work areas. Even chemical products that are shipped into a facility or redistributed to other containers must bear proper hazard labels.

Material safety data sheets (MSDS): An MSDS describes all the hazards associated with a chemical, how to handle and store the chemical, the proper personal protective equipment to use when handling the chemical, and so on. According to the Hazard Communication regulations, an MSDS must be maintained for all the chemicals at any given workplace, and it must be easy to read and readily accessible to all employees.

Training: Training is critical to make sure employees understand the hazards in their workplace and how to do their jobs safely. The Hazard Communication Standard requires employee training on all aspects of understanding and using the MSDSs.

In general, the Hazard Communication Standard requires businesses to have MSDSs for all potentially hazardous chemicals present at a work site. If employees use consumer chemical products in the same manner that a regular consumer would, *in small doses* as directed by the manufacturer, an MSDS is generally not required. On the contrary, if employees use consumer chemical products for purposes that extend beyond that of an average consumer — especially in regard to the frequency and quantity of use — then the exposure rate is higher, and MSDSs would be required.

Regulations continue to change

The EPA is not the only agency involved in researching air quality issues and the need for change. In 1972, the Consumer Product Safety Commission (CPSC) was created. This organization has become well-known for product recalls. These generally result from reported deaths and other serious consequences connected to specific product usage or misusage. The CPSC also evaluates the safety of household products and the chemical compound substances contained therein.

Many other groups continue to do research and make it available to the public. One such agency is part of the U.S. Department of Health and Human Services. They are known as the Agency for Toxic Substances and Disease Registry (ATSDR). The agency was created in 1980 to specifically deal with toxic environmental waste issues. In 1986, the Superfund Amendments and Reauthorization Act gave them more responsibilities concerning environmental public health issues. Although the organization is best known for its research concerning toxic substances polluting soil and groundwater and their resulting health affects, they also research indoor air quality.

The ATSDR continues to provide the public with information on updated research concerning the effects of chemical compositions in the home and workplace. The field of environmental research produces new studies daily. As additional data is collected, products require changes. As a result, more substances are banned or require restrictions. Companies are being forced to create newer safer products to comply with the regulations. The ATSDR provides detailed toxicology and health risk information about chemicals on their Web site. It is easy to use and understand; just type the hazardous substance name in the search box at **www.atsdr. cdc.gov/toxfaq.html**.

The "dirty dozen" and "nasty nine" are considered extremely toxic and have therefore become banned worldwide. But this does not mean that they are the only chemicals affected by government regulations. There are multiple agencies around the world researching chemicals and the resulting environmental and medical consequences involved in their use. For example, two other predominant substances, lead and phthalates, were restricted in 2008 as a result of findings reported by the U.S. Consumer Product Safety Commission (CPSC).

Consumer Product Safety Improvement Act of 2008

In August 2008, the CPSC dramatically enhanced existing product safety laws. The legal action came as a result of the Consumer Product Safety Improvement Act. This was the biggest change of its kind since the passage of the original Consumer Product Safety Act of 1972. The new legislation came about largely because of widespread bans on lead and phthalates and became effective immediately.

Phthalates — chemicals produced from oil — are widely known as having been used to make plastic products more pliable over the past 50 years. They have also been commonly used in other substances such as hairspray, lubricants, perfumes, deodorants, various beauty care items, and floor-finishing products. But they have also been linked with birth defects, kidney and liver damage, and reproductive problems. The ban on products containing phthalates went into effect in February 2009.

The ban on products containing lead deals with products used by children under the age of 12. Lead is actually a naturally occurring substance that does not break down. It comes from the earth, but like many other toxic substances, it can change properties when exposed to sunlight, water, and other chemicals. According to the ATSDR, people are exposed to lead through swallowing and breathing, and the substance has the potential to affect any organ in the body. The most concerning effect is the potential for brain damage. Children are more susceptible than adults because they are more likely to put things in their mouths that may contain bits of lead, such as paint chips, markers, and even clothing containing certain dyes. The Consumer Product Safety Improvement Act creates new standards for safety. It requires mandatory third-party testing procedures, product-tracking labels, and registration. It also provides the CPSC with a greater amount of control in maintaining these new safety provisions and requires that products for children must contain labels with updated warnings.

Precautionary Principle

As time goes on, more government agency studies reveal health and environmental risks posed by toxic chemicals in everyday items. Yet, despite all the data, regulatory action remains vague. Although some substances are banned, for the most part, companies are dictated by something called the "precautionary principle." Scientists, lawyers, policy makers, and environmentalists met in Wisconsin in January 1998 to summarize the principle. It states, *"When an activity raises threats of harm to the environment or human health, precautionary measures should be taken, even if some cause-and-effect relationships are not fully established scientifically."*

In other words, it places a lot of responsibility in the hands of the companies making the products. It also means consumers need to be aware of the current regulations as well as the potential dangers of continuing to use the products in their homes. This is particularly true for those individuals who suffer from non-descript symptoms that cannot be attributed to anything else.

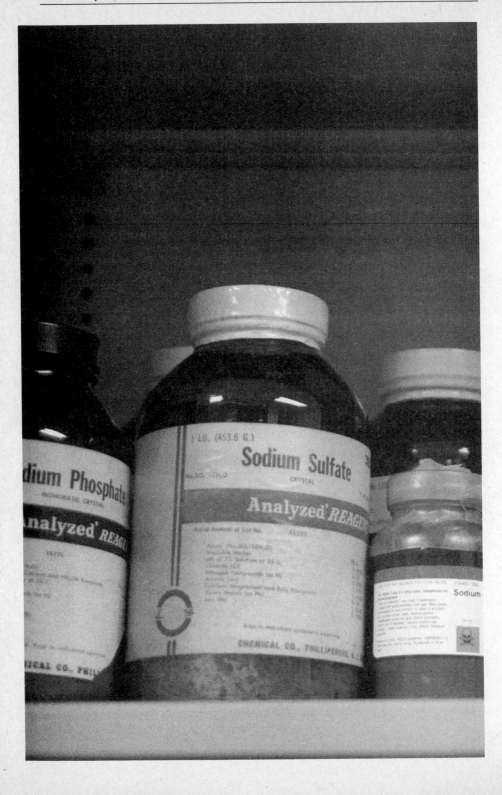

Chapter 2
The First Step

"The beginning is the most important part of the work."

— Plato, Greek philosopher

Identifying the Problem

First things first: Find out what you have at home now. Identify all the potentially harmful chemicals. If it is not a product that is toxic, make sure to follow the directions on the label. To be safe, wear gloves and open the window. This is particularly important in the areas you use the most cleaning products: the kitchen and the bathroom.

Chemicals are present throughout the home in many different forms. The easiest place to start is with the cleaning products you would normally keep away from children and pets. According to the American Association of Poison Control Centers, a child is accidentally poisoned every 30 seconds at home.

Mr. Yuk

The Mr. Yuk symbol was created in 1971 by a Poison Control Center inside of Pittsburgh Children's Hospital, located in Pittsburgh, Pennsylvania. It was devised to help children understand that there are certain products they need to stay away from. These specific substances are dangerous and should not be played with or consumed. The idea was to create a universal symbol that kids could understand.

Mr. Yuk stickers, with a distinctive bright-green cartoon face, are helpful in teaching children not to touch poisons or other unknown substances. Hopefully, as regulations continue to change, there will be fewer toxic substances in household products, and the stickers will become unnecessary. Until then, pay close attention to labeling on all the items you use in your home. When reading labels, notice how they are worded. There are certain words that are particularly important on any household product label, now known as a *warning label*. These words should never be ignored.

TOXIC	**Toxic** Toxic is not a good substance in any form. It means poison and could pose a problem for any family member, pet, or plant it comes in contact with.
DANGER	**Danger** This is a big clue. Danger means there is a possibility of harm or injury to someone or something that comes in contact with it.

	## Caution Caution is something you need to pay attention to. It is not as detrimental as "toxic" or "danger," but it needs to be used correctly. An example of a cautionary statement might be to use the product in an open, ventilated area, instead of an enclosed space because of fumes. Another example would be to make sure the product is not mixed (intentionally or accidentally) with another particular substance.
	## Flammable This indicates the substance can be easily ignited, will burn quickly, and may spread fast. In this case, keep the substance away from open flames, gasoline, and oil. Do not consume, and contact your local poison control center if ingested or if it comes in contact with eyes. These substances are usually poisonous.
	## Irritant This word primarily suggests there is a potential for some kind of skin or eye irritation if proper care is not used. In this case, gloves are a good idea, and users should be very careful not to touch their eyes while using the product. As a general rule, it is a good idea not to touch any area of the face while using any manufactured cleaning product.
	## Keep Out of Reach of Children This notion is self-explanatory. There are substances contained in the product that could be poisonous if swallowed. These should be kept away from pets as well.

Note: If an item has the words "caution" or "warning" on the label, pay attention. Here is something to think about: If a product has a color or a fragrance, some sort of chemical had to be added to make it that way.

The Federal Hazardous Substances Act

The Federal Hazardous Substance Act was enacted in 1960. The U.S. Consumer Product Safety Commission updates and maintains its information. The act demands very specific hazard descriptions on consumer product labels; manufacturers must provide details on all potentially hazardous substances. Potentially hazardous substances can be toxic, corrosive, flammable, irritating to skin or eyes, or have a composition that changes with heat or pressure.

The label details must also include specifics on correct usage and a list of cautionary measures to take should an emergency occur. Subsequently, the act necessitates chemical labeling if there is any chance of injury or illness resulting from reasonable handling and use of the product. It requires designation regarding precautions to avoid the possibility of accidental ingestion by children or pets. Labels must also include steps to take in an emergency, such as accidental ingestion or contact with the eyes and other mucous membranes. Furthermore, the act provides the commission with the ability and authority to ban a substance it deems extremely hazardous to consumers.

Housing an Arsenal of Chemicals

Houses are filled with chemicals. Some are obvious, such as medicine; some we take for granted, such as strong cleaning agents. The smell of bleach and ammonia means the house is clean, right? Wrong. Mixing ammonia and bleach results in a toxic, possibly fatal substance. The problem with using strong chemicals in the home is that you may unknowingly use it with another strong chemical and accidentally create something highly toxic — or even deadly.

Strong chemicals are not the only issue. There is also the pleasant aroma of air fresheners and scented candles. One of the most common substances used in making these types of fragrances is formaldehyde. The well-known embalming agent is also used in multiple household cleaning products, furnishings, and insulation in older homes. It is highly toxic and a known carcinogen, or cancer-causing agent, for animals. When you put all of the strong scents together, it can cause sensory overload, even for people not sensitive to the chemicals used in them. For people who are sensitive to fragrances, the result can be migraines. In worst-case scenarios, the EPA lists it as a possible carcinogen for humans as well.

CASE STUDY: HOUSEHOLD CLEANING PRODUCTS AND FRAGRANCES CAUSE MIGRAINES

Christina Peterson, MD
15259 SE 82nd Dr.
Suite 201B
Clackamas, OR 97015
503-656-9844
noheadaches@migrainesurvival.com

Dr. Peterson founded HEADquarters Migraine Management to fill the need for migraine education and awareness. She started a private practice in neurology in 1986, and is now the medical director of The Oregon Headache Clinic. She is also a member of the National Headache Foundation, the American Headache Society, the International Headache Society, the Headache Cooperative of the Pacific, and the American Academy of Neurology. Dr. Peterson is a reviewer for the journal Headache, *and occasionally participates in drug studies. She frequently speaks on the subject of migraines and other headaches to hospitals, employers, physicians, and nurses.*

For headache sufferers, especially those who suffer from migraines, the chemicals found in many cleaning products are headache triggers. These compounds cause headaches by providing chemical irritation to the nerve fibers in the nasal lining and branches of the trigeminal nerve. In migraine sufferers, it is the trigeminal receptors in the brainstem that affect the nerves and create a cascade of familiar symptoms. The most common trigger chemicals include:

- Fragrances
- Solvents, such as propylene glycol, glycol ethers, and other alcohols
- Irritants, such as formaldehyde and kerosene

CASE STUDY: HOUSEHOLD CLEANING PRODUCTS AND FRAGRANCES CAUSE MIGRAINES

These trigger chemicals enter the air in the form of volatile organic compounds (VOCs). Although many cleaning products are marketed as fragrance-free to appeal to headache or allergy sufferers, they may actually possess extra chemicals that mask the smell of strong chemicals.

The addition of fragrances to cleaning products is virtually unregulated. Despite that, some manufacturers admit to adding fragrances for consumer preference. Test results indicate that consumers value a pleasant smell over cleaning ability. If these same consumers were asked if they preferred a fragrance that caused headaches, ended up in wastewater, and harmed fish, would the answer be the same?

Some manufacturers are open about the chemicals they use in their products. They post their MSDS information online for public viewing. Other companies are less forthcoming about their product contents. One manufacturer proudly proclaims their dish detergent can clean oil off the wings of a bird, but they do not disclose the ingredients that evoke that cleaning power.

The other household product that is of particular concern to headache sufferers is laundry softener. In the form of fabric softener and dryer sheets, the chemicals and fragrances contained in these products may be big headache triggers, and are designed to stay on the fabric for days.

If you, or someone else in your household, suffer from constant headaches, consider looking at the chemicals you use in your home. Removing a substance is better than adding a medication.

There are many products you use every day, and you know they possess chemicals. But there are others you may not even be aware of. For example, there are toxins sprayed on clothes, furniture, and electronics. For years, chemicals have been applied to these items as flame-retardants. A flame-retardant is something applied to an item to keep it from becoming instantly flammable and spreading a fire to other areas too quickly.

Flame-retardants were originally invented to help provide safer cooling and insulating measures for industrial fluids. Early flame-retardant substances, known as polychlorinated biphenyls (PCBs), were used as far back as the 1920s. During the 1930s, Harvard University researchers published a paper depicting the hazardous nature of these substances, including the fact that over-exposure caused liver damage. Despite mounting evidence depicting liver and thyroid damage, as well as birth defects and neurological problems, PCBs were not banned until 1977.

PCBs were included in the original dirty dozen in 2001. In 2009, additional flame-retardant chemicals were banned. They are known as brominated flame-retardants (BFRs) and have been used in many electronic household items. They were developed to inhibit the possibility of combustion in electronic products and their housing devices. Unfortunately, they are also highly toxic.

This chapter provides specific information on how to look through the products in your home and help you determine what is potentially toxic. Some of substances listed have been banned for years. They are included here because they may linger on items in your home. For example, furniture, electronics, lighting, clothing, and even cleaning products exist in many homes for years.

Check Your Labels

Many toxic chemicals are found in household cleaning products and personal care items. Be aware of them in any form that comes in contact with your eyes, skin, mouth, or nasal cavities. If the product has been in your home for more than a year without use, get rid of it. *See Chapter 16 for more detailed information on product disposal.* If you want even more information on the products you currently you use in your home, you can research ingredients online. Information is readily available on the Internet, but be sure to use a reliable source, such as the Agency for Toxic Substances and Disease Registry (ATSDR) or the National Institutes of Health (NIH).

First of all, before you buy a product, check for cautions. That part of the label will give you a lot of information. If users are strongly cautioned, it is probably a good idea to find an alternative product. In addition to the statements of caution, there are important statements about usage. Always use the product exactly as it is intended. Product misuse has generated many calls to the Poison Control Center. The label should also explain what to do in terms of first aid. If not, do not hesitate to call Poison Control, or even 911, depending on the issue. Visit the National Capital Poison Center at **www.poison.org** and click on "Other Poison Centers," located on the left, to access your regional poison control phone number — there are 61 centers nationwide. Or, you can dial 1-800-222-1222 to be routed to your local center.

Newer labels may also contain information on disposal, given the concern for the environment and recycling. This is of particular interest. Not all plastic bottles containing chemicals are automatically recyclable with your other plastic items. Read all labels carefully; they are there to help keep you and your family members safe.

Putting it in Perspective

It is hard to believe that there are so many chemicals in the products we use every day. It is even more disturbing to realize the number of potential health conditions that could result from their usage. If one person uses a tiny bit of one cleaning product just once, that person is probably not in danger of contracting a horrible disease or ending up in a coma — but it is the culmination of product use and misuse over a long period of time that can create a problem.

The usage of multiple items simultaneously provides a good example of product overload. For example: Any one modern appliance used in moderation would not use an excess of energy, but consider a large family all at home on a hot summer day. The air conditioning is running full-blast, and three people are watching TV. Each is using a different TV because they cannot agree on what to watch. At the same time, two individuals are using computers connected to multiple mp3 players, and cell phones are being charged. The dishwasher and the washing machine are running. These activities take place over the course of several hours. Then, the microwave is used while someone is in the bathroom running a hair dryer. Suddenly, the power is out, and everyone wonders why.

This may be a funny scenario, but it is not too far removed from what happens in a typical American home. More importantly, it serves as an example of how multiple activities over time create a problem. Now, how does this pertain to chemicals in household cleaning products?

It has to do with many family members using dozens of chemical cleaning substances in the household. For example, a family who wants to clean the house before a big party will use many substances to clean. You break out the arsenal of cleaning products, and everyone is dusting and scrubbing in separate rooms. Your husband is working on the yard, adding fertilizer to the lawn and killing weeds in the garden. Your daughter is cleaning porch furniture with all-purpose cleaner. The bathrooms have been extra sanitized with bleach. It is really hot outside, so the air conditioner has been running all day. You set out candles and use air fresheners to tone down the chemical smells. You do not want to open the windows because the grass and pollen make your allergies flare up. To finish the day, everyone hits the showers and uses another arsenal of chemicals in personal care products: soap, shampoo, and deodorant. By the time the party starts, everyone in the house is exhausted. Additionally, everyone is complaining about headaches.

What could have caused the headaches and fatigue? Did everyone work too hard? Probably not — more likely, sensory overload caused those headaches. It was a culmination of all the products used together attacking the senses. Add to that the possibility of adverse conditions in the use of some of those products, and the fact that the kids may not have read the labels and they may have used incorrect amounts of the products. As a result, everyone ends up miserable. Of course, it is not as obvious as accidental ingestion, or burning skin, but it is a problem nonetheless. It is affecting the health of those surrounded by the multitude of chemicals used at one time.

All things in moderation are fine for the most part, but unfortunately, when left to our own devices, many of us forget moderation in the name of convenience. For that reason, making your own cleaning products out of non-toxic household items found in the pantry is a very appealing option. Most of the items are natural, ingestible, and inexpensive to use, making it a win-win scenario.

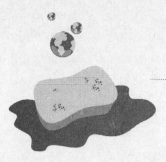

Chapter 3

What are the Options?

"Unless someone like you cares a whole awful lot, nothing is going to get better. It's not."

— Dr. Seuss, author

Determining the problem is only the first step. The next step is determining the available options. When deciding how to approach housecleaning in an eco-friendly manner, there are three primary alternatives:

1. Hire an eco-friendly cleaning service.
2. Replace toxic products with greener versions.
3. Make your own environmentally safe, non-toxic household cleaning products.

Hiring an Eco-Friendly Housecleaning Service

Many people work outside of the home and find the time for housecleaning a task that they do not have time for. If you do not have the time, hate the chore, and have the funds to do so, you may want to consider hiring a service to do the cleaning for you. Whether you are already using a cleaning service or decide to start using one for the first time, there are a number of things to question. If you are concerned with the effects of cleaning products on the environment and your family's health, you have the right to ask how the service will perform the cleaning tasks. If you are hiring a service for the first time, set up a time to interview the potential service either in person or over the phone. Here is a list of questions to ask:

- How long have you been in business?

- What do you charge? To determine what is reasonable, compare other services in your area.

- Are you bonded? If someone is bonded, it means that the employee has insurance through a bonding company that will cover any damages incurred, either intentional or accidental.

- Do you carry insurance for any problems that may occur? If you are employing a single person, rather than a well-known company who may be connected with a bonding company, you should ask if they carry this type of insurance to cover themselves. You should make sure that they are covered for damage and loss.

- How often do you come to the house, and what days are you available to come?

- How many customers do you currently have?

- Is there any flexibility in scheduling if I have something come up and need to change my allotted time, or have a function coming up?

- Have you ever had any customer complaints? If yes, what have they been?

- May I have a list of references? Make the effort to contact other customers and find out if they have been satisfied with the service. Remember to ask about the products that have been used and their effectiveness in other customer's homes.

- Do you provide any kind of guarantee for services provided?

In addition to the questions you would generally ask anyone coming into your home to do service, you should also ask about the cleaning products and equipment that they use. Here is a list of questions to ask:

- Do the business owners consider themselves to be an eco-friendly cleaning service?

- Do you bring your own products, or will you use products I have?

- If you bring your own cleaning products, what are they?

- Are the products and equipment you use considered environmentally safe? If you are unfamiliar with the products they will use, research the product names online.

- If the products are "green," what is their effectiveness in cleaning pathogens such as staphylococcus and E. coli?

- Is your company green-certified? If they use green products, they need to go through a certification process to receive a green seal of approval. Determine if each of the cleaning products has been certified.

The Green Seal Environmental Standard for Cleaning Services

Green Seal™ is a non-profit organization created to ensure standards concerning environmental sustainability were uniformly monitored in cleaning services claiming to be green. The organization maintains standards with strict adherence in order to achieve the Green Seal stamp of approval. They consider the logo to be the mark of environmental responsibility for products and services.

The group was founded in 1989 and maintains specific environmental standards for products and consumers. They first enacted product certifications in the early 1990s. Now, according to the Green Seal Web site, they have more than 40 categories for products that can be certified by the organization. They test and evaluate products on what is in the product, how the materials were obtained, how they are manufactured, what they are contained in, how they will be used, and what methods will be necessary for product and container disposal.

If a product has been evaluated by the Green Seal organization and received approval, the logo will appear on the product's label. When researching and interviewing cleaning services, you can ask if their business and their products have received the Green Seal stamp of approval. Information is also available on the Green Seal Web site.

Likewise, if you have a service or product you wish to have certified, you can visit the Green Seal Web site and follow the evaluation procedures, at **www.greenseal.org**. The organization institutes standards based on requirements determined by the International Organization for Standardization (ISO). The standards for obtaining Green Seal certification are broken down into the following categories:

- Home products and services
- Personal care and consumer packaged goods
- Construction materials, equipment, and systems
- Facility operations, maintenance, and services
- Hospitality, lodging, and food service
- Transportation and utilities

CASE STUDY: ECO-FRIENDLY HOUSECLEANING SERVICES

Shirley Forney
Owner, Shirley's Healthy Choice Housecleaning Business
76 Towpath Road
Duncannon, PA 17020
717-834-9362
sforney@hotmail.com

Shirley Forney has operated her own eco-friendly housecleaning business for four years. She believes in only using non-toxic, eco-friendly products. A year ago, she switched to using Shaklee products predominantly because they did a great job in her home and did not give her any headaches, as other products had in the past.

It is important to me to not only make things clean, but to do it in a responsible way. I started out using mostly eco-friendly products right from the beginning. My business partner used other products she was familiar with when we first started working together. She was always coughing while she was using her products, and a lot of the time I ended up with a headache. I finally convinced her to switch to eco-friendly products. Eventually, I started using the Shaklee products, and I have been using them for about a year now. I am really happy with the results. Before that, I used eco-friendly cleaning products from Melaleuca.

The Shaklee products are safe for humans and pets. They are biodegradable and come in recyclable containers. They also quality-test all of their items to guarantee the purity and safety of each product. It is my understanding that they are even using Shaklee cleaning products to clean the White House. One of Michelle and Barack Obama's daughters, Malia, has asthma, so they wanted the cleaning products to be non-toxic and eco-friendly. Michelle Obama has been known to champion asthma awareness.

CASE STUDY: ECO-FRIENDLY HOUSECLEANING SERVICES

In addition to using Shaklee's products, I sometimes use a combination of 1 part vinegar to 3 to 4 parts water along with a few drops of sink detergent to wipe down kitchen counters.

I believe in using eco-friendly products everywhere around the house. I even make my own weed killer by mixing 1 gallon of vinegar, 1 48-oz. box salt, and ¼-cup of sink detergent. It does a great job of killing weeds — just be careful not to spray it on any plants you do not want to get rid of. The mixture kills everything, but it does it without any harsh chemicals.

Replacing Toxic Products with Greener Versions

If you clean your own house, one of your options is to replace any of the toxic cleaning products you have with newer eco-friendly options that are flooding the markets today. During the first decade of the new millennium, concern for the environment made an impact on goods and services. Worldwide, people started to hear information regarding their product usage and actions, and how they left something called a "carbon footprint." Dictionary.com defines carbon footprint as "a measure of the amount of carbon dioxide produced by a person, organization, or location at a given time." There are tools on the Internet to assist individuals in determining carbon footprint information. The calculation is based on home product and lifestyle choices, as well as travel variables. For more information, refer to **www. carbonfootprint.com** and click the "calculator" box on the left to choose whether you want to calculate your business or your home activities.

Some companies started researching the effects of their products on the environment more than 30 years ago. Subsequently, there have been some eco-friendly cleaning product options available for several decades. As scientists produced more research and government regulations became stricter, existing cleaning product companies started to reevaluate their product lines as well. Today, many companies have put their chemists and marketing geniuses to work in redeveloping and repacking their products so they will be more environmentally friendly and healthier to use.

Many factors affect the creation of a product. Despite growing concerns for the environment, manufacturers still have to consider the cost of production. Since water is the universal solvent, marketing a product using terms like "eco-friendly" and "new greener formula" may only mean there is a higher percentage of water in the formula. Currently, these phrases are not regulated. Be careful not to be misled by the labels. The term "green" may mean the product is less toxic — or it may mean it has reduced or biodegradable packaging, recycled ingredients, was manufactured to produce little negative environmental impact, or has minimal artificial ingredients.

What remains to be seen is how the recession, which began in October 2007, will affect the marketing of these products. People are becoming more aware of toxic products, and their effects on human health and the environment. Eco-friendly products that work well, do not cause significant health problems, and do not pollute natural resources would be beneficial to everyone. The question remains: What will people be willing to sacrifice in order to obtain those types of products? Will people be willing to spend more or order products online, if that were the only way to obtain them? When it comes to economic downturn, it is uncertain whether cost and convenience are instrumental in people's choice of products. Just hearing that a product is better for the environment may not be a deciding factor.

There are options out there for people willing to do the research. As individuals become more educated on environmental issues and more products become available, labels will be even more important. Just putting the word "green" in front of a product does not necessarily make it good for the environment or your family. There are multiple symbols showing up on product labels that tell you more about the product than just a list of ingredients.

Be Aware of Mislabeling

Eco-friendly products and packaging get attention. Marketing executives use that information to their advantage. There are many ways to use terms loosely in advertising and packaging. Regulations prohibit false claims, but items do slip through the cracks. The U.S. Federal Trade Commission (FTC) handles this issue. In June 2009, the FTC charged the K-Mart® Corporation, the Tender Corporation, and Dyna-E International with making unsubstantiated claims that their products were biodegradable. The FTC produces guidelines on the interpretations of legal regulations. These guidelines are known as Green Guides. The guides inform marketing strategists that they may claim their item is biodegradable only if they have scientific evidence. The evidence must prove that with normal means of disposal, the product will totally decompose within a reasonably short amount of time. For specifics on word use laws, you may review the Green Guides online at the FTC's Web site: **www.ftc.gov/bcp/grnrule/ guides980427.htm**.

As the trend toward environmental responsibility continues to expand, many manufacturers are eager to join the cause. Unfortunately, as evidenced in the FTC case above, not all companies can substantiate their claims. There is a term for this in the marketing industry. It is called "greenwashing." Dictionary.com defines greenwashing as the dissemination of misleading information by an organization to conceal its abuse of the environment in order to present a positive public image. Fortunately, there are organizations set up to provide more information for consumers who want to discover the accuracy of marketing claims. One such organization is the EnviroMedia Social Marketing Agency.

EnviroMedia was established in 1991, and it communicates information that improves personal and environmental health to the public. In December 2008, during the UN Climate Change Conference, EnviroMedia announced the launch of the Greenwashing Index. The intention was to provide consumers with an area to discuss environmental product claims. The site includes ads that are the most authentic, as well as those that are deemed to be the worst offenders.

EnviroMedia partnered with the advertising faculty of the University of Oregon School of Journalism and Communication to create the Greenwashing Index Web site at **www.greenwashingindex.com**. The online forum allows consumers to judge the green claims made by major advertisers. It is intended to help consumers protect themselves from companies that spend time and money claiming to be green, but do not necessarily implement business practices that minimize environmental impact.

The Greenwashing Index is a mechanism for consumers to evaluate different ads. The index is a scale that allows grade ranging from "authentic" to "bogus," and everything in between. The University of Oregon School of Journalism and Communication's advertising program developed the criteria. Led by professors Deborah Morrison and Kim Sheehan, a group of students developed and chose five elements for consumers to use in order to analyze advertisements and decide on their authenticity. The criteria are:

- Misleading with words
- Misleading with visuals/graphics
- Making a vague green claim that is seemingly improvable
- Overstating or exaggerating how green the product/company/service actually is
- Leaving out/masking important information, making the claim sound better than it is

When people rate an ad with the Greenwashing Index, it generates a score based on the response to the criteria above. The score is included in the ad's overall score, and individual comments are added to the tally. High scores are undesirable.

The Design for the Environment (DfE)

The Design for the Environment (DfE) logo represents a program supported by the EPA. The DfE program works with representatives from industries and environmental groups to make positive improvements in products. Their goal is to evaluate products based on their effects on human health and the environment. They also take into consideration the materials used, transportation issues, processing, and the costs involved. According to the EPA, the program has already reached more than 200,000 business facilities. Additionally, they boast of their reduction of the use of dangerous chemicals by approximately 357 million pounds.

Some products are better than others. To determine what is best for you and your family, read labels and research products online. If convenience is an issue for you, and you prefer purchasing cleaning products (instead of making them), you may want to consider using some of the eco-friendly alternatives currently on the market. Below is a list of some of the more well-known eco-friendly cleaning products. Some of them are readily available in grocery stores and other chains; others need to be ordered online or through distributors.

Note: In the interest of research, Atlantic Publishing Group, Inc. provided me with funds to purchase and test a number of eco-friendly household cleaning products. However, Atlantic Publishing was not otherwise involved in the experimentations, the products I chose, or the results that I described. *I discuss my personal experiences with the specific products I chose in Chapter 4.*

The following descriptions mentioned here are merely some of the many eco-friendly products I came across in my research. The list is by no means comprehensive. It is also important to note that inclusion in this group does not mean these products are necessarily preferable to any other product out there. There are multitudes of choices. The information is intended to provide you with basic information on some of the products currently available on the market. Additionally, new products emerge every day.

Seventh Generation

 Seventh Generation™ is a Vermont-based company that has been around for 20 years. The company takes their name from the Great Law of Iroquois Confederacy: "In our every deliberation, we must consider the impact of our decisions on the next seven generations."

They have an extensive line of products that includes household cleaners, dishwashing products, laundry products, paper items, and feminine and baby care items. The products are easy to find in major grocery stores and Target®. They may also be purchased online. Check out their Web site at **www.seventhgeneration.com**.The Seventh Generation household product line includes:

- Fabric Softener Sheets
- 100 Percent Recycled Bathroom Tissue
- 100 Percent Recycled Napkins
- 100 Percent Recycled Paper Towels\100 Percent Recycled Facial Tissues
- Recycled Trash Bags

- Natural All Purpose Cleaner
- Kitchen Cleaner
- Natural Glass & Surface Cleaner
- Shower Cleaner
- Toilet Bowl Cleaner
- Tub & Tile Cleaner
- Carpet Spot & Stain Remover
- Natural Dish Liquid
- Automatic Dishwasher Gel
- Dishwasher Rinse Aid
- Automatic Dishwasher Pacs
- Natural 2X Concentrated Laundry Liquid
- Baby Laundry Liquid Detergent
- Chlorine Free Bleach
- Delicate Care Laundry Detergent
- Natural Powdered Laundry Detergent
- Natural Fabric Softener
- Natural Fabric Softener Sheets

Simple Green

Bruce Fabrizio and his father introduced Simple Green® products 30 years ago. Sunshine Makers, Inc. markets the product line. The line includes industrial and household products that are available all over the world. Simple Green products are also easy to find in all major grocery and hardware stores. There are also carried in numerous smaller stores. Visit their site at **www.simple-green.com.** Here is a list of the products that they carry for the home:

- All-Purpose Cleaner
- Lemon Scent All-Purpose Cleaner

- Stone Cleaner
- Stone Polish
- Stainless Steel One-Step Cleaner & Polish
- CAT Pet Stain & Odor Remover
- DOG Pet Stain & Odor Remover
- Deck & Fence Cleaner
- House & Siding Cleaner
- Concrete & Driveway Cleaner
- Paint Prep & Clean-Up Hard Surface Cleaner
- Paint Prep & Clean-Up Brush and
  Roller Cleaning Gel
- Paint Prep & Clean-Up Mold and
  Mildew Remover
- Pro Series Simple Green MAX
- Pro Series Simple Green GLASS
- Car Wash
- Pro Series Simple Green Scrubbing Pad
- Hand Cleaner Gel
- All-Purpose Wipes
- Lemon Scent All-Purpose Wipes
- Scrubbing Pad
- Heavy Duty BBQ & Grill Cleaner
- Bike Cleaner Degreaser
- Lime Scale Remover
- Carpet Cleaner

Although the regular Simple Green product line was eco-friendly, they decided to further to improve their products. They started a new line of products under the label Simple Green Naturals™. These products have all received Green Seal certification.

- Naturals Dish Washing Liquid
- Naturals Liquid Hand Soap
- Naturals Multi-Surface Care
- Naturals Bathroom Cleaner
- Naturals Glass & Surface Care
- Naturals Dilutable Concentrated Cleaner
- Naturals Floor Care
- Naturals Carpet Care

Nature's Source

Nature's Source™ products are part of a branch of S.C. Johnson & Son, Inc. products. The company currently markets four environmentally friendly household cleaning products under the Nature's Source brand. The items are all plant-based and made from 99 percent natural ingredients. They are available at all major grocery stores and discount store chains. The slogan for this new product branch is "Clean for your family. Green for the world." Learn more at their Web site at **www.naturessourcecleaners.com.**

The new eco-friendly products are:

- Natural Glass & Surface Cleaner
- Natural All-Purpose Cleaner
- Natural Bathroom Cleaner
- Natural Toilet Bowl Cleaner

Green Works

Green Works™ is a new line of products manufactured by the Clorox® Company. The products include eight all-purpose and bathroom cleaners and four laundry products. According to the Clorox Company, the green component is based on three major principles: Each product must be made from renewable resources, must be biodegradable, and must be free of petrochemicals. The EPA recognizes these products for their safer chemical composition. They also have the DfE seal of approval and are never tested on animals, contain no phosphorus or bleach, and are packaged in recyclable materials. See their site at **www.greenworkscleaners.com.** The product line includes the following.

- Natural All-Purpose Cleaner
- Natural Dilutable Cleaner
- Natural Bathroom Cleaner
- Natural Toilet Bowl Cleaner
- Natural Glass & Surface Cleaner
- Natural Glass Cleaner
- Natural Cleaning Wipes
- Natural Dishwashing Liquid
- Natural Laundry Detergent
- Natural Laundry Stain Remover

Jeff Campbell's Clean Team

Jeff Campbell's Clean Team℠ started as a three-person cleaning company in San Francisco. The company now offers a full-service product line, including cleaning tools and speed-cleaning tips. The products are non-toxic, biodegradable, odor-free, and environmentally friendly. They are made from all-natural ingredients, such as seaweed, soybean extracts, palm kernels, and palm oils, and contain approval ratings from the EPA, USDA, and the FDA. The products are available through a catalog or online at the company's Web site at **www.thecleanteam.com**. The cleaning product line includes the following:

- Red Juice

- Blue Juice
- Tile Juice
- Scum Bum
- Sh-Clean
- Pro Scrub
- Stainless Steel Cleaner and Polish
- Fiberglass Cleaner
- Chandelier Cleaner
- Furniture Feeder
- Marble, Granite, and Stone Cleaners
- Leather Forever Care
- Brass & Copper Polish
- Furniture Polish

Method

Method® is a private company started by two young men named Adam Lowry and Eric Ryan, who were roommates at Stanford University. Lowry is a chemical engineer with a degree in environmental science, and Ryan was in advertising prior to co-founding the Method Company. They started the company to create environmentally safer cleaning products that would be made without toxic ingredients. Their slogan is "Method creates products for people against dirty." The products are available online and in some drugstores. The line encompasses more than 100 products that are arranged in categories on the Web site by color and smell. The products are relatively popular, but they are not 100 percent natural. The Web site states that the functional cleaning elements are all made from 100 percent natural ingredients; the products are, however, enhanced by color dyes and fragrances. The items come in recyclable packaging. The products are available online and in many drugstores and grocery chains. The Web site is **www.methodhome.com**. Some of their household cleaning products include:

- Wood for Good Polish Duo
- All-Purpose Cleaner
- All-Purpose Cleaner Duo
- Bathroom Cleaner
- Tub & Tile Spray
- Le Scrub Bathroom Cleaner
- Lil' Bowl Blu Toilet Bowl Cleaner
- The Daily Granite Granite and Marble Cleaner
- Stainless Steel Cleaner
- Best in Glass Glass and Window Cleaner

Biokleen™

Jim Rimer started Biokleen in 1989. Rimer was a commercial cleaning products sales person. He believed that many commercial cleaning products caused serious, negative health effects, and it gave him the desire to create a non-toxic product line. The Biokleen product line includes industrial and household products. The household line consists of laundry detergents, sink and dishwasher detergents, and several general surface cleaners. Biokleen items can be ordered online or purchased in health food and other natural stores. Take a look at their site at **www.biokleenhome.com.** The household product line includes:

- Citrus Laundry (in powder and liquid forms)
- Free & Clear Laundry (in powder and liquid forms)
- Premium Plus Laundry Powder
- Chlorine-Free Oxygen Bleach Plus
- Cold Water Formula Laundry Liquid Energy Saver
- Hand Moisturizing Dishwash Liquid

- Automatic Dish (in powder and gel forms)
- Free & Clear Automatic Dish Powder
- Lemon-Thyme Dishwash Liquid
- Free & Clear Dishwash Liquid
- Lavender-Lime Bac-Out Bathroom Cleaner
- Citrus Essence Bac-Out Multi-Surface Floor Cleaner
- Spray & Wipe All Purpose Cleaner
- Bac-Out Stain & Odor Eliminator
- Ammonia-Free Glass Cleaner
- Soy Cream Cleaner
- Soy Toilet Scrub
- Citrus Soy Solvent

Mrs. Meyer's Clean Day®

Thelma Meyer developed the Mrs. Meyer's Clean Day product line. The items are made from natural, biodegradable substances and come in recyclable packaging. At **www.mrsmeyers.com,** the sitecites the following disclaimers concerning the natural ingredients:

"We use naturally derived ingredients whenever possible from corn, sugar cane, coconut, and palm. When we cannot find a plant-derived ingredient that performs to our rigorous standards, we use ingredients from the world of safe synthetics. These are materials with a long history of safety and efficacy in use for people and the environment they live in. At Mrs. Meyer's Clean Day, we do our best every day to make our formulations as natural as possible without compromising freshness and performance."

Regarding the term "chemical-free," the Web site posts the following statement:

"Honestly, this is an impossible claim to make. Water is a chemical, air is a chemical, essential oils are chemicals, and the world as we know it is a configuration of various carbon chains. The chemists at Mrs. Meyer's Clean Day are committed to making smart, responsible raw material choices and, whenever possible, obtaining materials from renewable plant resources such as olive, coconut, corn, and soy."

Much of the product line is touted as a "aromatherapeutic" and therefore does contain fragrances. There are 14 different types of scented household cleaners, four laundry items, and an array of products made specifically for babies. The items are available online and at a small number of health food stores and grocery chains. The household cleaning product line includes the following items:

- All Purpose Cleaner
- Surface Wipes
- Surface Scrub
- Countertop Scrub
- Window Spray
- Automatic Dishwashing Liquid
- Automatic Dishwashing Packs
- Dish Soap
- Liquid Hand Soap
- Room Freshener
- All Purpose Soap Bar
- Toilet Bowl Cleaner
- Shower Cleaner

Shaklee

Dr. Forrest C. Shaklee founded the Shaklee® Corporation in 1956 at age 61. Shaklee is best known for its nutritional supplements, but in 1960, the corporation produced a biodegradable household cleaner. Now they sell a number of eco-friendly household cleaning products under their Healthy Home Product umbrella. The Get Clean® starter kit includes 11 Shaklee cleaning products and 17 pieces of cleaning equipment. Shaklee is a distributorship program — in other words, the products are not sold in stores and must be purchased through an authorized seller called a distributor. Check out their site at **www.shaklee.com.** The basic household cleaning product kits include:

- Basic H2 Organic Super Cleaning Concentrate
- Basic H2 Organic Super Cleaning Wipes
- Germ Off Disinfecting Wipes
- Nature Bright® Laundry Booster and Stain Remover
- Scour Off™ Heavy-Duty Paste
- Hand Wash Concentrate
- Dish Wash Concentrate
- Dish Wash Automatic Concentrate
- Fresh Laundry Concentrate HE Compatible, Regular Scent or Fragrance Free Liquid
- Soft Fabric Concentrate
- Soft Fabric Dryer Sheets

Safer Detergents Stewardship Initiative (SDSI)

More companies are working to change their formulas and develop new products every day, but some companies are working more diligently on this front than others. For these companies, the EPA's Designed for Environment Program has executed the Safer Detergents Stewardship Initiative (SDSI). The SDSI recognizes industry leaders who voluntarily use safer surfactants. A surfactant is a substance that affects surface characteristics, such as foaming and lubrication. It is essentially a wetting agent, and is sometimes referred to as "wettability." It is a substance that decreases the surface tension of a liquid during its use. Companies that qualify for this award are given this seal of approval. In order to receive the seal, they must apply at the EPA Web site at **www.epa.gov/dfe/pubs/projects/formulat/sdsi.htm**.

The following companies received SDSI awards for their product formulations.

- Auto-Chlor® System
- Barricade Fire® Gel
- Bissell® Homecare Inc.
- Chemco® Corporation
- ChemLink Laboratories LLC
- Clean Control® Corporation
- Earth Friendly® Products
- Eco Concepts, Inc.®
- Georgia-Pacific® Consumer Products LP
- JohnsonDiversey®, Inc.
- Klipper Group
- Method
- A Henkel Company
- Multi-Clean® Inc.
- S.C. Johnson & Son®, Inc.
- Natural Soap Formulas
- Naturell®
- PDQ® Manufacturing
- VASKA®
- Virox® Technologies Inc.
- U.S. Polychemical® Corp.
- US Formula® Technology
- State® Chemical Solutions
- SafeWash® Technologies
- Pure & Gentle® Soap Inc.
- GEMTEK® Products LLC
- Reckitt Benckiser®, Inc.
- EcoDiscoveries®
- Seventh Generation, Inc.
- Corporate Express®, a Staples Company
- The Dial Corporation®
- The Procter & Gamble® Company
- SYSCO™ Corporation
- Spurrier Chemical Companies Inc.

Make Your Own Cleaning Products

According to market research, in 2008 Americans spent more than $400 million on all-purpose cleaners alone. That is only one type of cleaning product. The World Bank says Americans spent close to $69 billion in a year on all types of household cleaning products. But according to consumer product spending research, those numbers are not increasing. The question becomes: Is it an issue of the recession, or a byproduct of environmental awareness? Most people might not realize it, but they probably have almost everything they need to clean in an eco-friendly manner sitting in their kitchen pantry right now. Not the chemicals in plastic bottles stored in cabinets or under the sink — you will find cleaning products within items stored away in the food sections that are safe to eat and great for cleaning. Rather than spending money on cleaning products, you can combine certain items into self-made cleaning formulas. In some cases, you can even use many of them straight from the container. By doing so, you can keep your family safe from unnecessary health risks and end up saving money in the process. The chart below contains a general list of just some of the items you probably already have. It also contains some suggestions for basic household cleaning usages.

- **Baking soda:** cleaning agent, deodorizer, stain remover, drain cleaner, mild abrasive scrubbing agent, de-greasing agent, metal polisher
- **Cinnamon**: deodorizer
- **Club soda**: stain remover
- **Coffee grounds**: deodorizer
- **Cola**: drain cleaner, rust remover
- **Cornstarch**: stain remover, de-greasing agent
- **Cream of tartar**: mild, abrasive scrubbing agent
- **Garlic**: natural pesticide
- **Ice cubes**: solvent

- **Lemons/lemon juice**: deodorizer, disinfectant, de-greasing agent
- **Olive oil**: furniture polish, wood scratch repair, plant cleaner
- **Salt**: surface cleaner, weed killer, pesticide, scrubbing agent, drain cleaner
- **Vanilla**: deodorizer, mosquito deterrent
- **Vinegar**: cleaning agent, disinfectant, pesticide

Refer to Chapter 5 for additional information on how to make your own non-toxic household cleaning products. The chapter includes numerous tested recipes for all your household needs, including indoor and outdoor cleaning, lawn maintenance, and pest control.

Chapter 4

New, Greener Products Hit the Market

"It's not easy being green."

— Kermit the Frog, a Jim Henson Muppet

Given the changes in chemical regulations over the past two decades, manufacturers have reformulated many of their existing products. Even some companies whose products do not include banned substances have decided to be proactive in their attempts to make more eco-friendly cleaning agents. Consumers need to be aware of the options and know how to read the labels before making purchases.

As in the original versions of household cleaning products, always review the ingredients. If you are not familiar with the chemical names, read the cautionary statements on the label. The newer labels provide a good indication of how dangerous or toxic a substance is. This chapter describes some of the products currently being marketed as eco-friendly and includes information about the companies that make the products and reviews of the products themselves.

According to a study performed by Green Seal, the recession that began in 2007 and appears to be stabilizing toward the end of 2009 does not seem to have a great effect on the sales of greener products. Some people claimed to buy more eco-friendly products, while other said they were spending less on choices that were marketed as better choices for the environment. The study also stated that people were more likely to select brands they were familiar with in the long run, rather than basing their decisions on environmental claims. Most of the people who were contacted were not familiar enough with the information provided to understand the claims; therefore, they had a tendency to doubt the green factor in advertising.

Green Product Reviews

While preparing to write this book, I decided to research all aspects of eco-friendly cleaning. I read a number of books and articles, talked with government agencies and other organizations, and reevaluated my own eco-friendly household cleaning habits. In addition to making many simple changes in my own home, my family and I tested many recipes for home-made cleaning formulas. In order to truly cover all aspects of eco-friendly cleaning, I also researched the eco-friendly cleaning products currently on the market. To do this, my publisher reimbursed me for the variety of products I tested. This way, I had no bias toward companies that may have provided me with free products or compensation for positive reviews. It is also noteworthy to mention that I experimented in my own way; these methods should not be considered scientific. I tried to choose a wide variety of household products. The reviews below depict my personal experiences with these specific products. But there are many other good products currently available — this is merely a cross-section of available options.

Given that I have a family of five, laundry is my biggest household cleaning challenge. Laundry never goes away. When I started my product reviews, I decided to begin my research by testing environmentally friendly laundry options. Below is my personal review of the items I tested.

OxiClean®

OxiClean uses the slogan "powered by the air you breathe, activated by the water you drink." Orange Glo International makes the product. The company's team of scientists came up with a way to use oxygen in cleaning products ten years ago and have been very successful. With three children who play sports, I have to check for stains every time I do laundry. Since kids are not always the best at putting clothes in the laundry in a timely fashion, I am likely to find stains that may have been there for days. I used the OxiClean Spray-A-Way™ Instant Stain Remover, and I found it works better than any other stain remover I have ever tried. The ingredients are environmentally friendly and biodegradable, and the packaging is recyclable. OxiClean also makes a number of other stain-removal products. They are:

- OxiClean Max Force
- Multi-Purpose Stain Remover
- Versatile Stain Remover
- Triple Power Stain Fighter
- Spot and Stain Remover
- Baby Stain Soaker
- Baby Stain Remover

Arm & Hammer® Laundry Detergent

After the stains have been pre-treated, it is time to start the laundry. I tried two new environmentally friendly options, the first being Arm & Hammer Laundry Detergent. Baking soda is one of the safest substances to use in the house, as it is non-toxic and is a great cleaner and deodorizer. Arm & Hammer is known for their baking soda. I decided to try their eco-friendly laundry detergent. The product ingredients include baking soda and bio-degradable plant soaps, and the bottle states that it contains no phosphates or bleach. It is also highly concentrated, thus requiring using less product, and it comes in smaller packaging. It is easy to store and easy to lift because of the smaller bottle size, and it is also cost-effective: For about $3.50, you can clean 64 loads of laundry. Most importantly, the detergent produced clean laundry.

Wash-It Laundry Ball™

In my pursuit of eco-friendly laundry options, I stumbled upon something unique: the Wash-It Laundry Ball. I purchased a set of two for $7.49 at **www.amazon.com**. For that price, I figured it was worth a try. Each ball is made of recyclable plastic and contains numerous cleaning pellets. These pellets release ingredients throughout the entire wash and rinse cycle. They work through the activation of water molecules and ion exchange, which produces oxygen and hydroxide. The oxygen ion component is a natural cleanser. The product is completely hypoallergenic, as it does not contain any harmful chemicals or phosphates.

Each ball should last for 100 loads and is safe for all washing machine types and washable fabrics. It also claims to produce cleaner, softer laundry because a softening agent is built into the pellets. The enclosed pamphlet included with the Wash-It Laundry Balls states that the pellets in the balls kill odors and are effective on all types of stains. The test proved the claims to be accurate. I did 40 loads of laundry thus far, and there does not appear to be signs of the pellets dissipating yet. The clothes come out fresh and clean. If the ball indeed lasts for 100 loads, it would be much more economical than any liquid or powder detergent. The Shenzhen Become Industry and Trade Co., Ltd. in China produces the Wash-It Ball, and the company also carries a stain stick and a color booster product.

Seventh Generation

After the clothes were cleaned, I tried a couple of eco-friendly dryer products. The first came from the Seventh Generation line of products. Each container of Seventh Generation products contains a household tip or relevant fact about the environment. I tried the Fabric Softener Sheets.

The fabric softener sheets are made from 100 percent recycled paper. They have the look of brown meat packaging paper and are perforated throughout, which allow the consumer to use only what it is needed, eliminating unnecessary waste. Alternatively, I used one sheet multiple times with similarly positive results. Static cling was not an issue. The only possible downside is a lack of smell. As mentioned earlier, fragrance is something we are accustomed to, but it is not a necessity. In fact, the chemicals that produce fragrance are often toxic and frequent headache-inducers. If you prefer having a scent on your clothes and bedding, place one or two drops of essential oil on a rag and throw it in the dryer with the other items.

Mainstays™ Dryer Balls

Mainstays Dryer Balls are spiky plastic balls used in the dryer in place of fabric softener sheets. Regular dryer sheets are often toxic and non-biodegradable. Dryer balls are chemical-free, non-toxic, hypoallergenic, and reusable. Since the invention of dryer balls, many companies have come up with their own variations. The original version sells for $6.99 for a package of 2 through **www.amazon.com**. I purchased a pair under the Mainstays label at Wal-Mart for $2.49. The laundry balls essentially did what they promised. They helped with wrinkles, and static cling did not occur, which — in my mind — is the primary reason to use something in the dryer in the first place. There is no scent on your clothes and bedding, which could be a pro or a con, depending on personal preference. The only complaint

I have is that they are not very quiet: The balls bounce around against the walls of the dryer and can be loud at times.

Static Eliminator™ Dryer Sheets

 Static Eliminator Dryer Sheets are 100 percent hypoallergenic, reusable soft cloths that replace disposable dryer sheets. They can be washed once every three months to keep fresh, clean, and working. The cloth sheets do not contain any toxic chemicals.

The box states that the sheets safely eliminate static and wrinkles and softens clothes. There is, however, an occasional problem with static in larger loads of towels and bedding. The cloth dryer sheets are washable and should last for 500 loads in the dryer. According to the company, they will never spot or stain. They are also safe for all fabric types, including delicates. The Static Eliminator Dryer Sheets are priced from $11 to $24, depending on the vendor that you purchase them from. The company carries three other products as well. They are:

- Reusable Dusting Mitt
- Shock Stopper
- Pet Glove

In addition to trying the new eco-friendly laundry products, I tested a number of household cleaning products from a number of different vendors. Here are the results of my research:

Simple Green All-Purpose Cleaner and Lemon Scent All-Purpose Cleaner

Simple Green® products are non-toxic, biodegradable, non-hazardous, non-flammable, and non-corrosive. They come in recyclable packaging. They are concentrated so you do not need as much product, and you can dilute it with an amount of water needed for a particular cleaning job. I have actually been using Simple Green products for several years. We have two spray bottles that we bought in the beginning; now, we buy the larger 1-gallon container, fill up the spray bottles as needed, and just add water. It is a good product that is eco-friendly and produces great cleaning results. Be careful to follow the instructions: The concentrated formula is very strong and should not be used at full strength.

Nature's Source

According to the Nature's Source Web site, the S.C. Johnson & Son, Inc. Company has decreased greenhouse gas emissions by 15 percent and has eliminated more than 61 million pounds of volatile organic compounds from their use since 2001. Their products are simple, biodegradable, plant-based and more than 99 percent natural. I tested the Nature's Source Toilet Bowl Cleaner. To get a better idea of how well the product worked, I let the toilet bowl sit for a week unused. At that point, it had a moderate water mark around the rim. With no more than minimal effort, Nature's Source Toilet Bowl Cleaner got the bowl clean. It also had a pleasant, but not overwhelming, scent.

Green Works

Clorox® manufactures the Green Works product line. Since I was familiar with the Clorox name, I decided to test one of their new environmentally friendly products.

I tested the Green Works™ Natural All-Purpose Cleaner with the Simply Tangerine Scent, and the Green Works Natural Dishwashing Liquid. Both products worked very well and had a pleasant, but not overbearing, scent. The all-purpose cleaner was great at getting sticky food substances off the kitchen counter and removing residue from around the bathroom sink drains. But it was the dishwashing liquid that really impressed me. One 24-oz. container of the liquid lasted me for three months. Granted, I do use a dishwasher, but I use dishwashing liquid as well, a little bit each day. This product is extremely concentrated; it takes very little to get suds and get items clean. As a means of comparison, I planned to clean the inside of two trash cans, using the Natural Dishwashing Liquid in one and a generic dishwashing liquid in the other. It took two squirts of the Green Works product, compared to half of the other bottle, to achieve the same results. Given the limited amount of product needed to get results, I found this product to be economically and ecologically friendly.

Jeff Campbell's Clean Team

My neighbor suggested that I try Jeff Campbell's Clean Team products. I tested the Red Juice on my dirty kitchen countertops, and I was extremely pleased with the results. They were very clean, and there was no strong ammonia smell afterwards. The Blue Juice made my mirrors sparkle without the strong smell of ammonia as well. I was very happy with the results. Another thing that impressed me was their customer service — they have an unlimited money-back guarantee. Additionally, if you need to know how to clean something, you can call the number on the product bottle or Web site, and can reach an actual person to speak with. Not only that, but the person you reach knows exactly what he or she is talking about. The customer service representatives have knowledge and experience with their products.

My only concern involves the product names. If you use these products, be sure children understand that the products are only for cleaning. The names "Red Juice" and "Blue Juice" may tempt younger children. Otherwise, the products are very effective and reasonably priced. A 32-oz. container of Red Juice concentrate costs $14.95 and provides you with 20 full 16-oz. bottles of ready-to-use heavy duty cleaner.

Other household helpers: Microfiber cloth

Opinions differ concerning the exact origin of microfiber, but speculations include Japan, England, and Sweden. Regardless, microfiber is an accumulation of man-made fibers, including polyester, polypropylene, olefin, and nylon. They are very small — much finer than human hair. These fibers can absorb as much as seven times their weight in fluid. They are used in multiple products, such as cleaning cloths, mops, towels, basketballs, and sleeping bag insulation.

Microfiber cloths are eco-friendly because they can pick up dust, dirt, and grime without the addition of any cleaning products. Microfiber is also very effective if you care for it properly. You should not wash microfiber with other fabrics because it will pick up lint from the other fabric types.

I am big proponent of using rags for cleaning, as it eliminates the waste that comes from paper towel usage. Microfiber clothes, mitts, and dusters, are also excellent eco-friendly options. They are inexpensive and they can be reused frequently. They do not pick up lint, pill, or fray and withstand multiple washings. In testing different products, I purchased the Zwipes™ microfiber kit. All of the products clean without chemicals. They are also lint-free and streak-free. The kit includes:

- Microfiber Interior Detail Mitt
- Microfiber Magna Duster

- Microfiber Magna folding Duster
- 3 - Microfiber Cloths

The six-piece kit was inexpensive, at around $11. Although the marketing is gimmicky, the products are easy to use for all members of the family, and they work very well. According to the packaging, the 90,000 fibers per square inch allow the cloth to catch all that dust and dirt, and it holds up to eight times its weight in moisture if necessary.

Eco-Friendly Cleaning Elsewhere

Trends in eco-friendly housecleaning are not important to just homeowners; they also affect those in charge of cleaning public areas as well. Decisions are made daily concerning how to effectively clean schools, stores, businesses, and hospitals. The interesting part is that even hospitals are making the change toward environmentally friendly products. See the following Case Study for an example:

CASE STUDY: ECO-FRIENDLY HOSPITAL CLEANING

Janice Dunn
Manager Environmental Health
Penn State Hershey Medical Center
500 University Drive
Hershey, PA. 17033
Phone: 717- 531-5531
E-mail jdunn@hmc.psu.edu

Janice Dunn is the manager of environmental health at Penn State Milton S. Hershey Medical Center. They test multiple cleaning products on multiple surfaces before deciding to use it in the hospital setting.

The trend toward using environmentally friendly cleaning products is not only affecting homeowners. Businesses, schools, and even hospitals are re-evaluating their cleaning products in respect to environmental impact and toxicity.

A national not-for-profit organization known as Hospitals for a Healthy Environment (H2E) has created a nationwide movement for sustainability in health care.

CASE STUDY: ECO-FRIENDLY HOSPITAL CLEANING

The American Hospital Association, the U.S. Environmental Protection Agency, Health Care Without Harm, and the American Nurses Association jointly founded the organization. It has ten years of experience in helping health care facilities become more eco-friendly.

We test new products as they come on the market, but we use 99 percent Johnson Diversity products at Penn State Hershey Medical Center. We have used them for a long time, and they keep improving with each infection issue. I keep up-to-date on what new products are available — products keep changing. Currently, we are trying a couple of eco-friendly products made specifically for hospitals.

Environmentally friendly practices are becoming more commonplace in hospitals, but we have been using them at Hershey for years. We were actually a little ahead of the game. Although environmentally friendly practices are currently not mandatory in hospital settings, many hospitals are realizing that using these kinds of products are beneficial to patients, as well as the environment. We started using Johnson's products when they first came out years ago, and we have been very happy with the results.

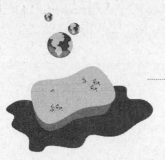

Chapter 5

Clean, Green Science

"All life is an experiment. The more experiments you make, the better."

— Ralph Waldo Emerson, American author

Chemicals are in pretty much every product on the market. Regulations are changing, and many companies are making a concerted effort to improve their products to make them safer and more environmentally friendly. If you are still concerned, the other option is to make your own products. This is not only a safe way to protect your family, but it is the most cost-effective. With just a few common household ingredients such as vinegar and baking soda, you can replace virtually all of your store-bought products. So, start experimenting with the formulas that appeal to you the most. I have listed several potential combinations below. Experiment until you find the combination that works best for you. Then make up a batch, put it in a sealed container, label it with the date, and store it in the cupboards. Because you are using primarily edible ingredients, you will not have to worry about Mr. Yuk anymore.

The following is a checklist of helpful items to gather before making your own cleaning products. This chapter also provides numerous formulas for creating cleaning products, and information on storing and labeling them.

Ingredients	Useful Tools
Vinegar	Funnel
Lemons	Measuring spoons
Lemon juice	Measuring cup
Table salt and coarse salt	Empty spray bottles
Baking soda	Bowls
Club soda	Mixing spoons
Cornstarch	Bucket
Cream of tartar	Soft cloth
Cloves	Toothbrush
Cinnamon	Blender or food processor
Garlic cloves	Pot for boiling ingredients
Hot pepper sauce	Clean glass jars with lids
Olive oil	Empty plastic containers with tight-fitting lids
Borax, found with other laundry detergent powders in the grocery store	Essential oils (optional for fragrance)
Washing soda, also found with laundry detergent powders in the grocery store	
Tap water	

Become a Home Scientist

Products that are marketed for mass use need preservatives and a certain amount of chemicals to maintain consistency and allow for a longer shelf life. They need to hold up during shipping and must be usable in different climates and environments. When you make your own products at home, this is not an issue. You can plan to make what you need for one day of cleaning or enough to store to future usage. Either way, use containers that seal and label them so you remember the formula for when you need to make more. There are many recipes available for making your own products. I have included the ones I tried and found to be successful. My children and I enjoyed being scientists and trying different variations to see what worked best. My suggestion is to use cheap, generic ingredients. For example, you do not need to use expensive Italian olive oil for making furniture polish. Save that for dinner. Buy whatever is cheapest, especially when you are experimenting.

Something to keep in mind: A favorite saying of people from the Depression era was "use it up, wear it out, make do, or do without." This is applicable today as well. While you gradually change out your chemical-laden cleaning arsenal, try some of these recipes for all-natural cleaning agents made from ingredients you already have in your home. They do require some elbow grease, but they are simple, eco-friendly, and inexpensive.

CASE STUDY: USING HOMEMADE CLEANING PRODUCTS

Jess Totaro,
Homemaker
Camp Hill, PA
E-mail: triathjt@juno.com

Jess Totaro is an environmentally conscious wife and mother. She has two children, ages 1 and 3 years old. As such, she has plenty to clean around her house and likes to keep things simple. She values products that are safe, efficient, and economically sensible. For that reason, she makes her own household cleaning products from completely safe, non-toxic ingredients.

For the majority of my cleaning needs in the kitchen and bathrooms, I use diluted white vinegar mixed with water. A simple mixture includes equal parts vinegar and tap water. If I want some scouring power, I spray the solution onto baking soda and make a little bit of a paste. I also make my own furniture polish using a combination of olive oil and lemon juice.

To make the furniture polish, you need a clean spray bottle. The recipe calls for

CASE STUDY: USING HOMEMADE CLEANING PRODUCTS

1 cup of olive oil and ⅓-cup of lemon juice. If you prefer, you can use the juice of five real lemons, squeezed into the bottle. Shake it well before using it.

I cannot remember exactly when I started making my own products, but it may have been after I read the *Queen of Clean®* books. I have been cleaning this way for a very long time now, and I cannot imagine ever changing back to purchased cleaning products.

There was a time when I did not use this method of cleaning — I used to be hooked on Lysol® and all means of other chemical products to clean, polish, and sanitize. I changed for two main reasons: I was concerned with the health of my family, and with the health of the environment. I know chemicals are bad for the environment, and it also bothered me to be using so many chemicals around my family, particularly with young children in the house.

I am very happy with the results I get using these safer, homemade products. My 3-year-old likes to help me do the cleaning. Since I use vinegar, baking soda, olive oil, and lemon juice, I do not have to worry about her getting them on her skin and getting a rash or a burn. I also do not need to worry about her accidentally swallowing anything, since all the products are essentially edible.

In addition to using vinegar, baking soda, lemon juice, and olive oil, I have another natural cleaning tip that I love: I regularly clean my garbage disposal by putting small pieces of orange or lemon peel down the disposal and running it. It freshens up quickly and easily. Plus, the smell of citrus is divine.

Formulas for Making Your Own Products

Here they are in recipe format. Decide what kind of product you are in need of, and examine the various options for making your very own concoction. Try out different ones until you find your favorites.

All-Star All-Purpose Cleaners

- Mix ½-cup of white vinegar with ½-cup of table salt. Stir until salt is dissolved. Use in spray bottle or on a sponge.

- Mix ½-cup of baking soda with 2 quarts of warm water. Stir to dissolve baking soda. Use on a sponge or soft cloth to clean countertops.

- Mix 1-½ cups of white vinegar with 1-½ cups of water. Use in a spray bottle on any surface.

- Mix ½-cup of baking soda into 1 cup of vinegar. Use as a paste anywhere you would use a soft cream cleanser.

- Mix ¼-cup of borax into 2 quarts of water. This is good for floors and countertops.

- Straight white vinegar works well on most surfaces as well. See Chapter 14 for cleaning temperamental surfaces.

- Mix 4 Tbsp. of borax into 4 cups of hot water until it dissolves. Add ½-cup of lemon juice for smell and put concoction in a spray bottle to use.

- Dissolve 1 tsp. of borax in 8 oz. of hot water. Add $1/8$-tsp. of liquid castile soap and shake vigorously. Put mixture in spray bottle for surface cleaning.

NOTE: Castile soap is considered an eco-friendly alternative to detergent soap products because it is made primarily from olive oil. It comes in solid and liquid forms and is a very popular, environmentally friendly option that is available through multiple vendors online. Some people even make their own castile soap. There are numerous different recipes for making this type of soap on the Internet.

Brighten-Those-Bricks Brick and Stone Cleaner

- Mix ½-cup of plain white vinegar in a bucket with 2 quarts of warm water. Use scrub brush on stubborn stains.

Crazy-for-Clean-Carpets Stain Removers

- Mix 1 Tbsp. of vinegar with 1 Tbsp. of borax and 1 Tbsp. of salt. Mix into a paste and rub into stain. Let sit until dry, and vacuum up residue.

- Mix 3 cups of club soda with 1 cup of hot water in a spray bottle. Shake well and spray on carpet stains.

Carpet Smells-Be-Gone Freshener and Deodorizers

- Mix 2 tsp. of cinnamon with 2 tsp. of ground cloves and 2 tsp. of baking soda. Sprinkle mixture on carpet and vacuum. The carpet with smell fresher, and the vacuum bag will hold onto the smell for the next room you vacuum as well.

- Mix 2 cups of baking soda with 1 cup of borax. Add 3 tsp. of lemon juice. Let it dry and sift all through powdered mixture. Shake onto carpet and vacuum.

Crystal-Clear Chrome and Stainless Steel Cleaners

- Dissolve 4 tsp. of baking soda in 2 quarts of warm water. Stir well, and use soft cloth to clean and polish finish.

- Make a cream out of 3 Tbsp. of baking soda and 3 Tbsp. of water. Rub creamy mixture over stainless steel area. Follow it by rinsing with club soda to eliminate any streaks.

Disease-Fighting Disinfectants

- Mix ½-cup of lemon juice into 4 cups of warm water. Stir in 4 Tbsp. of borax until dissolved. Pour into spray bottle for use as a disinfectant.

- Stir 3 tsp. of borax into 6 Tbsp. of vinegar. Add to 4 cups of warm water and shake well. Pour into spray bottle for use as disinfectant.

Dare-to-Shine De-Greasing Agents

- Mix ½-cup of washing soda into a bucket of warm water and scrub gently. This particular formula is good for most surfaces, but not recommended on aluminum or no-wax floors.

- Mix 1 cup of cornstarch with 1 cup of baking soda. Blot away excess grease with clean, uncolored cloth. Cover spot with the cornstarch and baking soda mixture. Let set to absorb grease, and vacuum or sweep away residue.

Delightful Deodorizers

- Mix ½-cup of baking soda with 1 Tbsp. of lemon juice and 2 quarts of water, and use mixture to clean out areas with odors, such as the refrigerator or trash can.

Destiny Improvement Dishwasher Detergent

- Place 1 Tbsp. of borax and 1 Tbsp. of washing soda in a sealed container and shake well. The complete mixture of 2 Tbsp. can be used for one full load of dishes in the dishwasher. Fill the rinse compartment with white vinegar. You can increase the amount of equal parts for future use. Make sure it is mixed well, and do not use more than 2 Tbsp. in the dishwasher. Cloudiness or powdery residue may appear on the clean items if you do not use vinegar.

- Baking soda can be used instead of washing soda. Again, the ratio is 1:1, mixed well with vinegar in the rinse cycle.

- Another alternative to this mixture is to add salt and citric acid. The combination helps with the residue issue, without having to add vinegar. The formula that works best calls for ¼-cup of borax, ¼-cup of baking soda, 1 Tbsp. of salt, 1 Tbsp. of citric acid, and about seven drops of essential oil. Mix well in an airtight container and use 1 Tbsp. of concoction per full load in the dishwasher. **Note**: Citric acid is a safe additive and may be purchased at grocery stores, pharmacies, and online at vendors such as **www.soapgoods.com.**

Dishwashing for the Future Liquid Sink Detergent

- There are not a lot of successful formulas for hand-washing dishes. I have tried some of the suggested formulas and found them to be messy and costly, requiring special ingredients. In my mind, this defeated at least part of the purpose. Therefore, I decided to try washing my dishes with vinegar and warm water. It worked. Add about 1-½ cups of vinegar to a sink full of dishes. The warm water and sponge does most of the work, and the vinegar acts as a disinfectant. If you have grime stuck to the plates, make a paste out of baking soda and water, and rub it on the caked on substance until it is removed. You can also add lemon juice for scent and degreasing. The best advice is to clean them right away, requiring minimal effort. The good news: All of these ingredients are non-toxic and safe to ingest.

Dreck-Dissolving Drain Cleaners

- Sprinkle drain opening with ½-cup of baking soda. Follow with 1 cup of white vinegar. Let sit for one hour, then follow with water to clear away clogs and remaining residue.

- Mix 1 cup of baking soda with 1 cup of regular table salt and ¼-cup of cream of tartar. Pour on top of drain and follow with 2 quarts of boiling hot water.

- Sprinkle drain opening with 1 cup of table salt and follow with 1cup hot water.

- Combine 1 cup of regular table salt with 1 cup of baking soda. Sprinkle above drain. Follow with 1 cup of vinegar. Mixture will fizz. Wait 15 minutes and wash through by pouring 2 quarts of hot water on top of the salt, soda, and vinegar mixture.

First-Rate Furniture Polish

- Mix ½-cup of vinegar with 1-½ cups of olive oil and shake in sealed container. Shake drops of mixture onto rag or other soft cloth and rub on wooden surfaces for dust-free shine.

- Mix 1 cup of lemon juice into 2 cups olive oil. Shake well and keep in sealed bottle, shaking well before each use. Pour small amount onto rag or other soft cloth and gently apply to wooden surface.

- Squeeze two or three drops of essential oil in a bowl of warm water. Mix well and dampen soft cloth. Gently rub on wood surfaces.

- Combine 1 cup lemon juice with 2 cups of regular vegetable oil. Shake well and pour a small amount on a rag or soft cloth to rub onto furniture. Using these ingredients, you achieve the shine and lemony scent of traditional furniture polish without filling your home with toxic chemical fumes.

Get-Grime-Out Grout Cleaner

- Grout cleaning requires elbow grease regardless of what you use, so use something that is cheap and easy — and that will not make you cough from the fumes while you are using it. One of the best concoctions I tried was a 3:1 ratio of baking soda paste. Mix 3 cups of baking soda with 1 cup of warm water and stir into a paste. Scrub onto grout with an old toothbrush for the best effect.

Living-Better Laundry Detergents

- Mix together ½-cup of borax and ½-cup of all-natural super washing soda and shake well in a container.

Note: Super washing soda is a natural detergent booster and freshener. It is similar in consistency to baking soda. Put an entire cup of powdered ingredients in washing machine. Mix in water before adding clothes for best results. You can make a larger amount of the detergent using these ingredients at a 1:1 ratio. Because it is a powder, you can store a large amount in a sealed container indefinitely.

- Grate one bar of castile soap into shavings. Melt 1 cup of soap shavings in 2 cups of boiling water. Mix together 1 cup of borax powder and all-natural super washing soda. Gradually add powdered mixture and stir well. Add 1 gallon of tepid water and mix well. Use ¼-cup of this concoction per full load of laundry and stir well before each use. For best results, add to water before adding clothing.

Marvelous Metal Polishes

- To remove tarnished surfaces on aluminum, brass, bronze, and copper, dip a half of a fresh lemon in a shallow dish of baking soda. Rub the dipped lemon all over surface to get rid of tarnish and improve shine.

- Mix 2 Tbsp. of flour with 2 Tbsp. of regular table salt and add 2 to 3 Tbsp. of vinegar to make a creamy paste. Rub on metal surfaces and let stand for one to two hours. Rinse with warm water and buff with a soft cloth. This works well on bronze, copper, brass, and pewter surfaces.

Magically Safe Mildew Removers

- Mix 1 cup of vinegar with 1 cup of salt. Apply to mildewed area and let it sit for one hour. Use scrub brush to work off residue.

- Mix 1 cup of borax into 2 cups of warm water. Once it is dissolved, add 1 cup of vinegar and stir well. Apply with sponge.

- Mix 1 cup of vinegar with 1 cup of warm water in a spray bottle and spray on mildewed area. Let set for one hour, then use scrub brush to get rid of mildew.

Magnificent Mold Removers

- Mix 1 cup of hydrogen peroxide with 2 cups of warm water in a spray bottle, and spray directly on moldy areas. Let sit for one hour, then use scrub brush to remove mold.

- Create a paste out of 2 cups of baking soda and 1 cup of vinegar. Mix the paste well and scrub onto moldy surfaces. This may be repeated if necessary.

- Fill spray bottle with 4 cups of warm water and 6 drops of tea tree oil. Shake well and spray on moldy areas. This works particularly well in the shower. Be vigilant about spraying mold as soon as you notice it. Mold is toxic.

Outstanding Oven Cleaners

- Most new ovens are self-cleaning, but if yours is not, or if you want to want to save power for environmental or economic reasons, you can mix 1 cup of baking soda with ½-cup of water to make a creamy cleanser. Use on a sponge to scrub off cooked on dirt. Note: If you do this before the oven is totally cooled, it is a little easier to get caked-on messes off. For particularly tough spots, rub baking soda mixture into grimy areas and let sit overnight. Wipe away with damp cloth in the morning.

- For ovens with extra caked-on grease, mix 2 cups of baking soda with ½-cup of all-natural super washing soda and add warm water to form a creamy cleanser. Smear on greasy areas and let it set overnight. Wear gloves, and use a rag and warm water to wipe off dried mixture the next day.

Play-it-Safe Pesticides

- Put eight cloves of garlic and 2 tsp. of hot pepper sauce into a food processor or blender until the mixture is liquefied. Stir mixture into 2 quarts of warm water. Put in a spray bottle and shake well before each use.

- In a blender, add 4 tsp. of freshly ground cloves to 2 quarts of warm water and pour into a spray bottle.

- Add eight cloves of garlic to eight jalapeno peppers and 1 cup of warm water, and mix concoction in a blender or food processor until liquefied. Add mixture to 2 quarts of warm water and put in a spray bottle for use.

- Place two entire bulbs of garlic and 12 small onions in a blender or food processor with 1 cup of warm water. Add 2 Tbsp. of red crushed pepper and blend until liquefied. Stir into 2 quarts of warm water and pour mixture into spray bottle.

Respectable Rust Removers

- Sprinkle coarse salt on top of rust. Coarse salt is larger grained than regular table salt. Kosher salt or sea salt may also be used. Squeeze juice from fresh lime or lemon over salted area and let it set for several hours. Wipe clean with soft cloth.

- Mix together 1 cup of fresh lemon juice and ½-cup of borax. Rub mixture onto rust stain and let it sit for 1 hour. Remove remnants and rust with soft cloth.

- Sift together 2 tsp. of cream of tartar with 2 cups of baking soda. Add 1-½ cups of hydrogen peroxide to form a paste. Put mixture on rusted area for one hour, then rub off with soft cloth.

Shinier Surfaces Silver Polishes

- Mix 1-½ cups of baking soda with ½-cup of water to form a paste. Rub onto silver in circular motion with soft microfiber cloth or rag.

- Mix 3 cups of water with 1 cup of cornstarch. Make into soft paste and rub onto silver items to clean.

- Mix 1 tsp. baking soda with 1 tsp. of regular table salt in a sink full of warm water, about ½-gallon. Dip silver pieces in and rub residue off with a soft cloth.

- For deeply tarnished sterling silver, place a small sheet of aluminum foil in a deep baking pan. Sprinkle the foil with 1 Tbsp. each of regular table salt and baking soda. Fill the dish with warm water and dip silver pieces in. Buff them with a soft rag, such as a baby's clean cloth diaper.

Treat-it-Right Tile Cleaners

- Make a paste out of 2 cups of baking soda and 1 cup of water. Mix until it is the consistency of a cream. Rub over tile and grout with a soft cloth.

- Mix ½-cup of vinegar with 4 cups of warm water in a spray bottle. Spray on tile. Use a squeegee to run over tile to clean. This can be done once a week with this mixture. Do not use straight vinegar on grout because it may break down the grout over time.

Trustworthy and Trendy Toilet Bowl Cleaners

- Put plain white vinegar in squirt bottle. Squirt up under rim of toilet edge and around water line. Follow by sprinkling toilet bowl with baking soda. Let sit for 20 minutes and scrub off with toilet cleaning brush. Flush to clear bowl when complete.

- Mix 2 cups of borax with ½-cup of lemon juice and pour into toilet bowl. Let it sit for 20 minutes. Scrub sides with toilet brush, and flush to clear bowl when finished.

- Mix 6 Tbsp. of baking soda with 3 Tbsp. of olive oil and 3 tsp. of lemon juice. Mix well and put in a squirt bottle. Squirt liquid under the rim of the bowl and along the water line. Let it stand for two hours and scrub with a toilet bowl brush for best results. Flush to clear the bowl.

Watch It Sparkle-and-Shine Window and Mirror Cleaners

- Mix 6 Tbsp. of vinegar with 2 cups of water in spray bottle for window mixture. Vinegar also works very well without adding water, but this makes the vinegar last longer and cuts down on the smell for sensitive noses. The vinegar smell does dissipate after about five to ten minutes, but if you or family members are particularly sensitive to the smell of vinegar, you can add 1 tsp. of any extract, or two drops of essential oil.

- Dissolve ½-Tbsp. of cornstarch in 2 cups of warm water. Add 1/8-cup of vinegar and shake well in a spray bottle.

Wipe-that-Wood Floor Polish

- Mix a bucket of 2 cups of olive oil and 2 cups of vinegar. Mix well and apply to floor with soft cloth or mop.

- Mix a bucket of 2 cups of vinegar with 2 cups of warm water and 1 Tbsp. of liquid castile soap. Use with mop or soft cloth and air-dry.

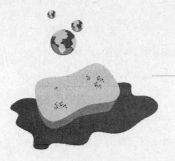

Chapter 6
Where to Start

"Start where you are. Use what you have. Do what you can."

— Arthur Ashe, tennis player

Household Basics

Organization and simplification

Before you start any new project, you need to get organized. Start by getting rid of anything you do not need. The fewer items you have sitting around the house, the fewer things you will have to clean. If this seems overwhelming, choose one room at a time and concentrate on that. Breaking things down this way makes them seem much easier to tackle. Since most of us probably have things we can live without, try living with less. It will simplify your life and your cleaning process. Consider asking yourself the following questions:

- Is this item something I really need?
- What function does it serve?

- Is it absolutely necessary, or just something I like to have?
- Is this the right place for it?
- How often do I use it?
- Is it something that requires special handling or cleaning?
- If I do not need it, what are my options for getting rid of it?

As you go through each room, have bins or bags available for sorting. If that is not feasible, at least designate sorting areas. Group items accordingly:

- **Goes in another room.** Sort by the room the items belong in.

- **Belongs to someone specific.** With multiple family members in one house, belongings are often misplaced. This is particularly true during the school year with papers and projects. Keep one bin per person, so as you clean, there will be one place for all the extraneous items left behind. This is an interesting practice because it helps you see who is predominantly responsible for leaving the most things behind. Then, you can address that issue as well.

- **Do not need it — Save for garage sale.** If your neighborhood has garage sales regularly, keep a bin somewhere out of the way in the basement or garage to save things for the sale.

- **Do not need it — Plan to donate it.** Goodwill is one option, and donations are tax-deductible. There are many other worthy organizations as well, perhaps a local church, homeless shelter, or the Red Cross. If you are not sure, ask around. My family recently purged a bunch of extra stuffed animals. Goodwill was not willing to take them, but the local YWCA had a program for domestic abuse victims. They took the stuffed animals for the children. Make sure anything you donate would be something you would want to receive.

- **Do not need it — Know someone else who might want it**. As you are scaling down your possessions, stop to think if there is anyone else you know who might want what you are getting rid of. Is there a family member who would cherish the item? Is there a friend who might like what you are getting rid of? If you have a number of items in this group, consider hosting a swap meet. Enlist friends and neighbors to bring out items they do not need, and swap them for things you do need. Be careful with this option. Make sure that if you do swap out your items, you only select new things that you really need. You do not want to just end up with more items to be sorted again next month.

- **Repurpose it**. Items sitting around the house not being used currently could be used for something else. For example, old, ripped clothing beyond repair make great cleaning rags. Jars that previously held candles can be used to store pencils and other office supplies.

- **Recycle it**. Plan accordingly. Is it paper? Is it plastic? Do I have a bin for it, or do I need to take it somewhere special? This would be the case for items such as paint, electronics, and phone books. *For specifics, see Chapter 16: Taking Out the Trash.*

- **Trash it**. Have a trash bag ready. No need to make extra work. If it goes in the trash, do it right away, assuming it cannot be recycled in some other way.

Once you have gone through every item in the room and determined whether it is really wanted or needed, have a plan to promptly get rid of items. You do not want to be sorting through these items again later next week.

After the sorting process...

Preparing to sell via consignment

You have sorted everything into piles. Take the next step and get rid of as much as you can immediately; there is no need to continually sort through the same items. First, have family members take their objects and put them away. Evaluate the number of items that are sellable. If you only have a few items, consider taking them to a consignment shop. For example, there are consignment shops for clothing, furnishings, baby-specific items, and other items. Check the phone book for stores in your area. These places take your possessions on consignment and give you a percentage of the profits after they are sold. Generally, the amount of money is determined by the length of time an item sits in the shop.

Hosting a yard or garage sale

If you complete the sorting process and find that you have numerous unnecessary items you are ready to part with, consider holding a yard or garage sale. Depending on the area you live in, and the season of the year, this may not be an immediately feasible option. If you need to plan for an event that is several months away, start by designating a storage spot in your home. As you encounter items you are willing to discard, put them in the storage area until closer to the date of the sale.

The most successful sales generally occur in neighborhoods that plan them together. Enlist the support of people who live nearby by passing out fliers or knocking on doors. Decide on a date and time, and stick to it. It can be a single-day event, or it can be held over multiple days. Advertise in the local newspaper, weekly shoppers, and local bulletin boards. Make sure to note items of interest, such as furniture, bikes, baby equipment, clothing, and so on. Have all participants pay a percentage toward expenses. If you do not live in a neighborhood, look into other organizations that host community yard sales, such as churches.

Prepare items by organizing them by category. Place similar items together, such as clothing in bins, and group them by gender and size. Items can be priced individually with stickers. Alternatively, similar objects can be clustered together with a single sign. For example, a table of books could be in marked with a sign saying 2/$1. You can earn a nice amount of money from big-ticket items, such as furniture, electronics, and antiques. Neatly presented, well-organized displays tend to be profitable as well.

Time to swap

If you participated in a group event, consider swapping items with other sellers, but only for something you really need. Certain items may also be swapped or traded in the retail environment: video games, computer games, handheld electronic system games, CDs, DVDs, and books. Check individual stores for rules. Some offer cash; others offer credits toward store items; and others simply swap items for others items in the store.

Donate the remains

After the sale is over, resist the temptation to take the remaining possessions back into your home. Plan to donate everything else. Place remaining items in bags or boxes and determine how and when you will get rid of them.

There are many organizations that take donations. Some groups stock the items and give them to those who are victims of a tragedy, such as a fire or flood. Some associations sell donated items and use the profits for those in need. There are many affiliations in the United States that take donations. Some examples are Goodwill, the American Red Cross, and Volunteers of America. If you have a local drop-off site and a small amount of remaining items, put them in bags or boxes and load them into the truck of your vehicle. That way, you can drop the items off the next time you pass the drop-off location. If you have larger items, such as furniture, or if you not have the ability to transport your remaining possessions, consider calling the local Volunteers of America office. Many offices in the United States will pick the donation up from your home. Find out more information about contacting your local Volunteers of America office at their Web site, **www.voa.org**.

Tools of the Trade: Eco-Friendly Household Helpers

The most important thing to remember in respect to cleaning equipment and appliances is taking care of what you have. If you take special care of something, it will likely last longer. Constantly replacing items such as appliances and tools is hard on the family budget. It is also not very good for the environment. Landfills are full of products people have either broken in haste or abandoned for something better.

When you actually need to look into new equipment, one of the key concepts of eco-friendliness is reusability. Try to get away from the idea that everything you use can just be thrown away. Instead of disposability, consider items that have longevity.

Vacuums and vacuum bags

The most eco-friendly flooring option is flooring that can be cleaned without electricity. However, since the 1950s, mass production of wall-to-wall of carpeting provided a prominent floor covering for homes in the United States. Sixty years later, the majority of houses in America are still carpeted to some degree. While area rugs can be shaken or beaten outside, wall-to-wall carpeting requires using some sort of vacuum cleaner. Vacuum cleaners by nature are not very eco-friendly. They are noisy, made of non-recyclable parts, and without the proper filter, throw dust and allergens back into the air we breathe. Therefore, use the vacuum sparingly. You can save wear and tear on the machine by picking up big pieces by hand.

If you are not in the market for a new vacuum, then make use of what you have. There is no need to be wasteful. If you do need another one, consider the following: The most eco-friendly vacuums use less power and last longer. When researching machines, look for a product that only serves what you need — an appliance that has enough power to get the job done. A few well-maintained carpeted areas in your home do not necessitate an industrial-strength vacuum.

If you decide to buy a new machine and you look into one that has a filter, make sure the filter is washable. If you purchase a machine that requires vacuum bags, determine whether it can use recyclable bags. If you consider investing in a deluxe vacuum cleaner that will last for years, you may want to consider one that has a High Energy Particulate Air (HEPA) filter. These filters are designed to filter dust particles that are down to 0.3 microns in size. To put that in perspective, one micron is equivalent to 0.000039 of an inch. For example, the eye of a standard hand-sewing needle is 749 microns wide. This filter will eradicate even the smallest particles and allergens from the carpet. The HEPA filter is reportedly almost 100 percent efficient in accomplishing this task. Industrial companies previously used them to get rid of lead and asbestos. They are now available for regular home use. They are particularly popular with people who suffer from allergies.

The mighty mop

Many people use their vacuums for the whole house, including non-carpeted areas. Wood, tile, vinyl, and other man-made flooring options really do not need to be vacuumed. They can be swept and mopped just as efficiently, which everyone did before the invention of the vacuum cleaner. Additionally, mopping and dusting can be done without the use of any special products. Over the years, as we tried to improve everything, people started adding soap and chemicals to every cleaning routine. However, either dry mopping or damp mopping with just a little bit of water is the most effective. If you mop this way, you will not have to worry about using a product that could damage your floor. There are now various specific types of cleaners for every type of flooring and surface. If you purchased all of them, you could end up needing a storage unit just for cleaning supplies.

In considering the type of mop to purchase, consider the material it is made from. Wooden handles and cloth handles are biodegradable, but cloth head attachments that can be removed and washed are even better. As with everything else, when looking at mops, remember the concept of reusability. For example, mops with microfiber heads that can come off and be washed would be considered one environmentally friendly option. Anything that can be used efficiently and cleaned easily is a wise choice. Also consider whether the product is made from renewable resources. Some synthetic items are not recyclable and are non-biodegradable, making them less eco-friendly.

To increase the lifespan of your mop, be sure to keep it clean, dry, and cared for. After you finish using the mop, soak the head of the mop in a bucket of clean, warm tap water and 1 cup of salt. Let it soak overnight. In the morning, rinse the salt solution from the mop and squeeze out any excess fluid. Hang the mop on a wall rack to dry. Make sure the head is off the floor to keep it from accumulating dust and mildew.

The basic broom

Prior to 1797, brooms in America were made by hand. People used whatever they could find to sweep away dirt: tree branches, twigs, brush, bamboo, straw, hay, and even cornhusks. Sometimes, these elements were used alone; other times, they attached them to longer sticks. These early sweeping mechanisms were not very effective, and they did not last very long. In 1797, a Massachusetts man named Levi Dickenson used sorghum crops to make a broom for his wife. Sorghum is a variety of upright grass plants grown for their stems and seeds. The variety pictured is sorghum vulgare, also known as broomcorn. Brooms are still made from this plant today.

During the course of the last century, manufacturers have invented many other sweeping devices that mimic the broom concept. Since the 1960s, manufacturers have tried to make alternatives to the traditional broom-corn broom. Modern brooms, made from numerous synthetic substances, such as plastic and rubber, come in many different shapes and sizes. The synthetic brooms are less expensive, but they tend to slide across the dirt, rather than holding onto it, making them ineffective.

Broom lovers believe that broomcorn brooms are the best brooms to use. Broomcorn stalks absorb dirt and dust while being moisture-resistant. They can also last about ten years if they are cared for properly. These brooms are the most expensive of the manufactured brooms, because many of them are still hand-made. These brooms are eco-friendly and work very well. When you are not using the broom, store it bristle-side-up to keep it in the best shape. This allows the fibers to dry.

Decent dusters

Vacuums, mops, and brooms all eliminate dust on hard-surface flooring. Vacuums are easy and convenient. They can be used for carpeting, furniture, and hard-to-reach crevices. Vacuums, however, require electricity, making them the least eco-friendly option. Brooms and mops work well on flooring, ceilings, and walls.

Other alternatives include dusters. A duster is a household-cleaning device used to remove dust easily from objects. It generally consists of some type of feather, fabric, or other material attached to a small handle. Users can easily manipulate dusters to gather dust off surfaces. They work on the principle of static electricity, allowing the duster head to attach to dust particles for easy removal.

The most common type of duster is the feather duster. Housewife Susan Hibbard fought her husband for the patent of the original feather duster, and won credit in 1876 as the inventor. Her idea stemmed from wanting to reduce waste in turkey preparation; she fashioned the first feather duster from turkey feathers.

Real feather dusters are generally made from ostrich feathers, a practice that dates back to 1903. A South African broom factory manager named Harry S. Beckner first used ostrich feathers to clean the machine parts in the factory. Beckner chose these because ostrich feathers' shape creates static electricity, making them excellent dust collectors. Beckner and his brother started the first feather duster company in the United States in Massachusetts in 1913, and this type of feather is still used in duster production.

Ostrich feathers are soft, flexible, and durable. They are safe to use on all surfaces because they do not scratch, and they can clean items like breakable collections and computer keyboards. It is also important to note that the birds are not harmed to gain the feathers, since they are gathered during the molting process. Ostrich feather dusters can be cleaned and maintained for many years. To care for them, shampoo the feathers and hang them tips-down to dry.

Other imitation feather dusters are not as efficient. Similar to the issue of the basic broom, synthetic materials used in producing dusters are cheaper, but inadequate. They slide over surfaces or propel the dust back into the air, rather than eliminating it.

Cleaning with cloth

In addition to using vacuums and an array of other handled items to dust, many Americans use paper towels covered in dusting spray. Irvin and Clarence Scott founded the Scott Paper Company in 1879 in Philadelphia, Pennsylvania. The president of the company, Arthur Scott, created the first roll of paper towels in 1931. Several years later, the concept caught on and gradually, disposable paper towels replaced the use of cloth towels in the home. Paper towels are convenient, but not very cost-effective. They are also not very eco-friendly.

According to the EPA, Americans use more than 85 million tons of paper and paperboard products each year. Of that, approximately 3,000 tons of paper towels are thrown away daily. According to Jennifer Kaplan, founder of Greenhance LLC, switching from paper towels to cloth could save you more than $100 each year.

There are many variables of paper towels production. Some companies are making paper towels at least partially out of recycled materials. Using recyclable materials is an eco-friendly concept, but considering the energy involved in production and transportation, they are still not the most environmentally friendly alternative. Additionally, most paper towels end up in the trash can, not a recycling bin. Many have been bleached to make them white, too, and you end up with more toxic items ending up in the landfills. If you consider the environmental mantra "reduce, reuse, recycle," paper towels are not the best option.

The simplest ideas are often the best ones, such as the original concept of cleaning with washable rags. You can take something you already have and repurpose it: Cloth diapers, old worn-out towels, mismatched gloves or socks, and discarded T-shirts all make excellent rags. Soft fabrics that will not mar or scratch surfaces are imperative.

Microfiber cloths are currently a popular option. Microfiber is synthetic substance made from petrochemical remains. A microfiber is tiny fiber with less than one denier, a measurement term that applies to the fiber count of individual threads, per filament. The threads are known as filaments. The denier count of an item expresses its durability, in respect to material in question. In respect to microfiber, the denier count denotes softness. For example, the Zwipes® products previously mentioned possess 90,000 fibers per inch. The size of the fibers allows the material to pick up small particles, such as dust, easily and effectively — without water or other products. It is also completely washable and reusable. With proper care, microfiber cloths will last for years.

The newest trend in eco-friendly cleaning cloths is the production of items made from natural sustainable fibers like hemp and bamboo. Bamboo is considered favorable because its fibers are bacteria–resistant. Hemp is a coarse plant fiber that has been around for years, and technological advances allow the production of softer hemp alternatives. The fiber has natural anti-bacterial and anti-fungal qualities, making it a positive alternative to man-made fibers. Using bamboo and hemp plant is more popular, but it is still an expensive alternative to making rags out of items you already possess.

To sponge or not to sponge

Cloth rags can be used to clean virtually anything. In certain cases, such as washing dishes, cleaning the tub, or scrubbing the grill rack, you may prefer something with a more abrasive quality. If you cannot live without sponges and scrubbers, there are a few environmentally friendly options.

Sponges are a species of colorful underwater animals that grow in a way similar to plants. There are more than 5,000 different varieties of sponges, and they are often used for cleaning because of their large porous surfaces that absorb liquids. The real sponges used for bathing and cleaning come from the creatures' skeletons. The animals can live about 20 years, then divers harvest the dead organisms. The sponges are cleaned and, in some cases, bleached or dyed before being sold.

European and Mediterranean cultures were the biggest natural sponge users. Natural sponges absorb well, last a long time, do not retain odors, do not stain as the polyester counterparts do, and are also used by artists. Most commercial sponges are synthetically made, predominantly from nylon and rubber, and are not biodegradable. These sponges can carry a lot of bacteria, which can be eliminated by rinsing the sponge with warm water, squeezing out the excess, and placing it in the microwave on high for two minutes and allowing it to completely cool before using. Do not use this method on sponges that are synthetic or contain metal. According to the United States Department of Agriculture (USDA), this significantly decreases the amount of bacteria that lingers on the sponge. Alternatively, you can place your sponge in the utensil compartment of the dishwasher each time you run a full cycle. This will eliminate almost all of the germs.

There are some types of natural biodegradable sponges on the market. The most common natural sponge, the cellulose sponge, is made from wood pulp, and comes in a variety of shapes, sizes, brands, and price ranges. In addition to sponges, there is a wide array of other scrubbing mechanisms on the market: loofah scrubbers, crocheted pads, and hemp scrubbers. Some manufacturers make scrubbers out of walnut shells, which is a very eco-friendly option since they are completely biodegradable and are not harsh on the hands the way pumice and plastic are.

CASE STUDY: ALTERNATIVES TO TRADITIONAL SPONGES

Mallory Whitfield
New Orleans, LA
www.MissMalaprop.com

*Mallory Whitfield writes about handmade and eco-friendly products and independent artists and designers on her Web site, **www.MissMalaprop.com**. She also designs recycled clothing and accessories. She lives in New Orleans, Louisiana.*

When my boyfriend and I moved into our current apartment, all newly renovated with the latest in eco-friendly features, it made me realize it was time to get serious about doing away with some of my less than eco-friendly regular purchases.

We typically used the universal yellow and green dish sponges around the kitchen for washing dishes and wiping countertops. We would have to toss them out every few weeks once they got grimy and disgusting. Finally, I came across these great handmade dish scrubbers and washcloths made by Laksaware on Etsy, a site for handmade products. (**www.laksaware.etsy.com**). They are machine washable and very affordable, at only $3 a piece.

I ordered a couple, and they have been such a lifesaver. You can just toss them in the wash with your dirty laundry to get rid of the daily grime. The hand-knit texture actually helps a lot with scrubbing dried-on food particles. That had been my main reason for not using a regular dish towel for some dirty kitchen jobs — sometimes the cloths are just too smooth to get off the crusty stuff. These scrubbers do their job, plus I find them easier to hold than a bulky dishtowel when washing the dishes, since they have a handle.

We fill up our automatic dishwasher and run it for most dishes — that is the most water-efficient way to go. But there are always some dishes that just need to be done by hand, and these handmade dish scrubbers do the trick.

If you can crochet, there are many simple patterns on the Internet for making your own scrubbers in a variety of shapes and sizes. Some of them even include directions for using recyclables, such as grocery netting or plastic bags. Below are directions for making a simple, straightforward circle scrubber.

Making a Circular Scrubber

In order to crochet a circle, start with a small loop. Increase the number of stitches each time you crochet around the loop. By increasing the number of crochet stitches in a simple pattern, you end up with a crocheted flat circle. Follow the following pattern to make the scrubber. You can use any size yarn and crochet hook.

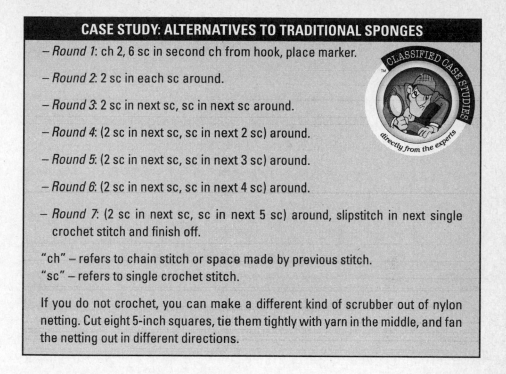

CASE STUDY: ALTERNATIVES TO TRADITIONAL SPONGES

- *Round 1*: ch 2, 6 sc in second ch from hook, place marker.

- *Round 2*: 2 sc in each sc around.

- *Round 3*: 2 sc in next sc, sc in next sc around.

- *Round 4*: (2 sc in next sc, sc in next 2 sc) around.

- *Round 5*: (2 sc in next sc, sc in next 3 sc) around.

- *Round 6*: (2 sc in next sc, sc in next 4 sc) around.

- *Round 7*: (2 sc in next sc, sc in next 5 sc) around, slipstitch in next single crochet stitch and finish off.

"ch" – refers to chain stitch or space made by previous stitch.
"sc" – refers to single crochet stitch.

If you do not crochet, you can make a different kind of scrubber out of nylon netting. Cut eight 5-inch squares, tie them tightly with yarn in the middle, and fan the netting out in different directions.

Grab a bucket

A good bucket is a housecleaning necessity. It is used for cleaning floors, cars, and various outdoor spaces at your residence. Make sure to invest in a solid bucket that will last for years. Most metal and plastic alternatives are recyclable, making them eco-friendly. Some less expensive plastic buckets, however, do not hold up well. Wooden buckets are another alternative. They are eco-friendly because they are biodegradable, but they may not be as watertight as their metal and plastic counterparts. Additionally, they may harbor mold and other bacteria over time.

Contain Your Enthusiasm — Or At Least, Your Cleaning Supplies

In addition to your cleaning tools, you may want to designate a variety of containers for your cleaning supplies. If you are making your own cleaning products, you may want to invest in some sturdy squirt bottles and some bottles with spray handles. They are available in most discount department store chains. If you would rather use what you have, you may carefully clean out the existing cleaning product containers in your home. Make sure to research the disposal regulations in your area. There may be rules regarding dumping chemicals down the drain, as they may end up in the water supply. *For more information on chemical disposal, see Chapter 16.*

If you have an empty cleaning solution bottle, but it contains a strong chemical smell that does not seem to go away with regular soap and water, try mustard. Mustard is great at removing odors, even those as strong as skunk smell. To remove the chemical smell from the plastic bottle, squeeze about 2 Tbsp. of mustard into the bottle and fill it about three-fourths of the way with hot water. Shake vigorously, then dump the contents. Rinse the mustard out, and the smell will be gone. This will work on any plastic container with a strong smell.

Besides bottles, you may also want set aside a variety of tubs or bowls with lids, and jars with vent holes. There are many simple eco-friendly house-cleaning tasks you can perform with single ingredients like baking soda and vinegar. For that reason, it makes sense to set aside separate containers of these products that are designated for cleaning and cooking. Tubs can hold dry ingredients, such as baking soda. Empty salt and powdered sugar shakers can hold ingredients like baking soda and cinnamon. The vented lids make them viable options for sprinkle deodorizers and other homemade air fresheners. If you do not already have these items, you can repurpose a clean glass jar by poking holes in the lids.

Get Others Involved

When making changes, it is easiest with support and encouragement. To make the transition go more smoothly, involve everyone in your household.

If you live alone, tell other friends and family members about your plans for change. Teach everyone what you are doing and, more importantly, why you are doing it. Show family members how to read the information on the labels of various products you have around the house. Help them realize what the different toxic substances are and the potential harm they could cause. Once you have improved everyone's awareness, enlist their help in finding ways to improve the situation.

- **Be a scientist**. Family members can help you try various recipes to make your own products. Children will find this activity interesting and fun. My children are particularly fond of cleaning the entire sink and tub drains with baking soda and vinegar because of the chemical reaction. It is fun to watch the two substances react by bubbling and fizzing. If you do not have children, you can still enjoy the science experiments yourself, with a significant other, or with a group of friends.

- **Become a tester**. Try the formulas in Chapter 5. Do a test to see which products and results you like best. Get creative. Try a bunch of recipes and make it a contest: One day might be about all-purpose cleaners. Which concoction cleans the best? What did you like about? How did it smell? How did the surfaces look and feel after they were cleaned? Is there anything you did not like about the substance?

- **Try something new**. Teach everyone about the various properties of household ingredients. Have them read the boxes to understand what it is supposed to do. After you have tested some of the formulas in Chapter 5, see if anyone can come up with their own. Turn family members and friends into chemists, and make it into a competition to see who comes up with the best recipe of their own.

- **Pick an ingredient**. Have everyone see how many uses they can come up with for using a substance, such as vinegar or vanilla.

- **Have a party**. If you live alone, or have difficulty getting support from family members, enlist some help from your friends. Decide to have a cleaning party. Invite some friends over to test some products. Offer to take turns doing the same thing at each other's house. Cleaning is much more fun with others helping.

- **Have a recipe swap**. After you and your friends have experimented with some of your own formulas, have a recipe swap. What recipes for cleaning products work the best? Write them on recipe cards and swap them with friends.

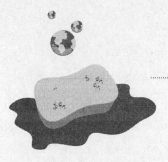

Chapter 7

Working From Top to Bottom

"Understand from top to bottom what the effort requires."

— Bill Toomey, 1968 American Olympic decathlon gold medal winner

Air Quality

In keeping with the theme of working from top to bottom, consider the overall air quality first. The first two chapters of this book addressed identifiable chemicals that are sprayed and rubbed on surfaces in the form of cleaning products. But there are also many unperceived toxins in your house. Most carpeting, furniture, and clothing have been treated in the stores, primarily with flame-retardants and stain repellents. Regardless, these are additional chemicals in your home. Add that to the normal dust particles and toxins that come into the house from outside on people's shoes, clothing, and skin. The various particles float through the air, landing on clothing and furnishings, thus affecting the overall air quality in your home. By reducing the number of toxins and particles in your home, you can improve the air and help everyone breathe better. A larger amount of foreign substance particles in the air greatly increases the chance of breathing problems, such as allergies and asthma.

The EPA states that the air inside our homes is highly toxic due to the numerous products we use every day. One of the common mistakes people often make is trying to freshen the air inside their homes by using air fresheners and disinfectants. Air freshening products actually use very toxic chemicals that create a layer of oil inside nasal membranes. In fact, the chemicals have a desensitizing effect.

Rather than masking odors by adding additional toxic fumes, use non-toxic, common ingredients to dilute odors and filter the smells. Here are some simple things you can do to improve the overall quality of the air in your home.

Test for Invisible Hazards

Radon

Many household toxins are odorless and invisible to the eye, making them even more dangerous. One of the most dangerous of these is radon. Radon is a gas that comes from the radioactive decay of radium. It is present in phosphate rock and many other common minerals. It becomes a problem in homes when it seeps through the ground and enters the home through cracks and crevices. The decay process releases particles into the air that mix with dust and can pass into lung tissue with normal breathing. Over time, breathing in radon can cause lung damage, cancer, or even death. Simple, low-cost, at-home test kits are available at retail hardware stores and other discount chain stores. If you prefer to hire a professional, you can check the EPA Web site for a certified professional. For more information, see **www.epa.gov/radon/radontest.html**.

Asbestos

Asbestos is a naturally occurring mineral that was commonly used in insulation and other building materials. Although the substance is no longer used in new construction, it still remains a problem. Older homes, workplaces, and school demolition and renovations create a risk of exposure. The deterioration of asbestos-based materials also poses a threat.

In addition to asbestos in building materials, some parts of the United States have naturally occurring asbestos (NOA). This is a certain type of mineral found in specific rock formations. Weather and human interaction can cause NOA to break down and infiltrate the air.

Like Radon, asbestos is a known carcinogen. Because dust from asbestos is primarily inhaled, the greatest health risks involve the lungs, such as lung damage or cancer. Asbestos experts should perform any testing if you are concerned. For state-specific information concerning asbestos testing, containment, or removal, review the EPA Web site at **www.epa.gov/asbestos/ pubs/regioncontact.html**.

Carbon monoxide

Carbon monoxide is another hazardous gas that affects homes. It is odorless and colorless, making it very difficult to detect. It has been nicknamed "the silent killer" because it often kills people quickly in their sleep without being detected. The symptoms mimic the flu: fatigue, headaches, dizziness, and nausea. Carbon monoxide detectors are available in most stores. Additionally, the EPA Web site lists the following steps you can take to minimize your risk of exposure:

- Keep gas appliances properly adjusted.
- Consider purchasing a vented space heater when replacing an un-vented one.

- Use proper fuel in kerosene space heaters.

- Install and use an exhaust fan vented to outdoors over gas stoves.

- Open flues when fireplaces are in use.

- Choose properly sized wood stoves that are certified to meet EPA emission standards. Make certain that doors on all wood stoves fit tightly.

- Have a trained professional inspect, clean, and tune-up central heating system (furnaces, flues, and chimneys) annually. Repair any leaks promptly.

- Do not idle the car inside the garage.

Lead

Another toxic substance common in homes is lead. The toxic metal was used in many products found in and around homes for years. It exists in and around older homes in paint, dust, and soil. It also poses a health risk in air and water. Lead is emitted into the air from motor vehicles, heating elements, and deteriorating paint. It enters drinking water through lead-contaminated plumbing materials. Health risks from lead exposure are most serious for young children. They include learning disabilities, neurological problems, seizures, and death.

Be aware of these and other potential hazardous substances that can pollute the air inside your home. The EPA posts detailed information about all pollutants, their sources, and the health risks on their Web site: **www. epa.gov**. News and other pertinent changes to regulations are updated on the site regularly.

Identify Biological Contaminants

Biological contaminants include bacteria, airborne viruses, pollen, mold, and mildew. They can accumulate in damp areas, or those that contain stagnant water. Open containers in the yard, gutter, air ducts, drain pains, and humidifiers are all sources of theses contaminants. They create a variety of health risks ranging from minor to severe. They include sneezing, congestion, watery eyes, rashes, coughing, muscle aches, nausea, chest tightness, fever, and chills.

Mold

Mold is a type of fungus that grows on plants, fibers, and other damp surfaces. According to the Centers for Disease Control and Prevention (CDC), the exact number of mold species is unknown. Scientific estimates suggest anywhere from 10,000 to possibly more than 300,000 different species of mold. For someone who is sensitive to mold, it is particularly harmful to human lungs. Symptoms can range from mild, such as sniffling and coughing, to severe in cases of obstructive lung disease.

Mold is a not new contaminant — it has always existed, and biologist Charles Darwin published a work concerning vegetable mold growth in 1881. It exists virtually everywhere and can grow on any organic substance. All molds are problematic because they are difficult to get rid of and are extremely troublesome to those who are sensitive to it. Mold allergy symptoms include sneezing, congestion, watery eyes, rashes, coughing, asthma, and wheezing.

Over the last decade, mold has become newsworthy, especially in reports on how toxic mold has caused serious illnesses and claimed a number of fatalities. However, only a small percentage of molds grow indoors. According to the Toxic Black Mold Information Center, only about one-tenth, or 16 of 160, of the known species of molds cause health problems in humans. Unfortunately, most of the molds that grow indoors are in this category. Many of them are considered allergenic, pathogenic, or toxic.

Once mold grows, it is very difficult to totally eradicate. The best thing you can do is to take steps to prevent it from growing in the first place. Excessive moisture is the general culprit: When water accumulates on surfaces without being removed, it provides the perfect condition for mold growth.

The best solution is to eliminate areas of potential stagnant water. Here are some suggestions for eliminating standing water sources around your home:

- Check all pipes and fix those that leak immediately.

- Check gutters, spouts, and drains. Make sure no water is pooling around these areas because of drainage problems.

- Check trash receptacle lids and be sure they are tightly closed. Do not leave trash cans or other open containers in the yard where they can gather standing rainwater.

- Empty the water pan in the dehumidifier promptly. After emptying the pan, clean it out with soap and water before using it again.

- Do not over-water plants. Leaves and soil can suffer from mold growth.

According to the American Lung Association, molds may even form on foam pillows from perspiration. If you are particularly sensitive to molds, you should take steps to prevent this, such as placing your pillows in an airtight cover and taping the cover shut. Wash your pillow every week in the washing machine, and dry it on the hottest setting until it is completely dry. The association also suggests replacing pillows once each year.

Wipe up water spills quickly. Keep your shower pulled closed at all times; a bunched shower curtain can harbor moisture. Additionally, use ceiling fans in bathrooms. Finally, replace moldy areas of carpeting and flooring so they do not spread. For more information on mold and mold removal, review the EPA Web site at **www.epa.gov/mold**.

Mildew

Mildew is very similar to mold, as they are both types of fungi, and the terms are often used interchangeably. Both organisms are spore-based and grow in moist places, but the main differences are the colors and textures. Mold is usually black, blue, green, or red, while mildew is generally gray or white. The other primary difference is the areas they affect. They can grow in the same areas, but mildew is more commonly found in the shower and on paper and fabrics. If food is affected, it is most likely mold.

As with mold, preventative measures are beneficial — good ventilation is the best remedy. Both mold and mildew are commonly found in bathrooms because of the increased moisture. Mildew tends to grow in dark, moist areas. In addition to bathrooms, it often appears in closets, attics, and basements. Mildew grows easily on natural fabrics that are wet; they smell musty and become discolored. In particular, cotton, silk, wool, and leather are common growth spots for mildew.

Use Proper Ventilation

Virtually everything emits gases somehow. Given the number of items in a typical home environment, it could easily become filled with air pollutants. An improperly ventilated area can increase the problem and expand the potential health risks. Even outdoor air can contribute to indoor air pollution. For example, exhaust from motor vehicles, heating and cooling systems, and building fans can all enter home through cracks, vents, and other openings.

The best thing to do in respect to improving the air quality is to air the house out by opening your windows. It is particularly important to keep the windows open during the cleaning process. This allows fresh airflow in and helps prevent the toxins from settling.

Additionally, open up interior doors. It is a good idea to keep general air flowing through the house as you clean. Even when you are not cleaning, this is a smart thing to do. If you do not like having the windows open all day, try to at least have them open for part of the day or night. Even a couple of hours each day will dramatically improve the air in your home. For the most part, homes today are very well-insulated. This is good for heating and cooling. On the downside, it also keeps all the toxins locked in.

Minimize unnecessary toxins

Minimizing the amount of toxins polluting the interior of your home will help. This includes everything from introducing fewer caustic substances to your home to watching the dirt that enters your home.

- **Use less-toxic cleaning products**. Changing to greener versions of products is a place to start. If you are unable to do that, at least water down the products you use. Water is a universal solvent. The products will still work, but you will be lessening the potential health risks. You do not need to make radical changes to make a difference. The other alternative is to use completely non-toxic substances, such as vinegar and baking soda, to perform the majority of your cleaning tasks. By using fewer toxic substances, you decrease indoor air pollutants and allergens.

- **Create a "shoes-off" policy**. Shoes carry dirt and other various pollutants on their bottoms. Having everyone take their shoes off and leave them by the door minimizes the amount of pollutants traveling through your residence. It also makes cleaning up easier, as less dirt will get tracked in on flooring and carpeted surfaces. Consider designating a special space for shoe storage. A bench, chest, or other low storage unit can neatly store shoes. A unit that provides a seating area for putting shoes on is even better. If you have a garage or mudroom, you can insist that everyone enter the house through those areas.

- **Designate an area for coats, boots, and sports equipment**. Besides being a source of pollution, these items tend to gather more dirt in general. If they are left outside or by the door, it minimizes the amount of cleaning you have to do everywhere else. Less vacuuming and floor mopping means less work for you. It also means you will need to use fewer cleaning products. Fewer cleaning products means less chemicals, so this concept eliminates multiple air pollutants.

- **Limit pet access to certain areas**. Many people will read this and think it is a ridiculous idea. That is certainly an understandable opinion. Pets are often considered to be members of the family and are therefore given the run of the house. This may be enjoyable, but they do increase in-home pollutants. They carry more dirt, germs, and insects. Furry pets shed, and pets in water tanks increase the chances of mold and mildew. If you are able, limit pet access to areas away from bedrooms.

Filter out excess pollutants

Even if you are vigilant in minimizing dirt, debris, and toxic substances, you cannot eliminate everything from the air inside your home. There are ways to effectively filter and purify the pollutants that do enter your residence.

Clean or replace filters. Filters on your heating and cooling systems can be taken out and hosed off regularly. Air filters are often dirty if they are properly working; after all, the function of an air filter is to collect and remove dirt particles from the air you breathe. When filters are extremely dirty, though, they can no longer remove particles. Conversely, they may actually release more dirt to enter your residence.

Heating and air conditioner filters should be cleaned once a month for optimum performance. If you suffer from allergies, have pets, or run your central heating and cooling unit day and night, you should consider cleaning the filter once a week. Hosing off or vacuuming standard filters can clean them. Some units use disposable filters, and you should not attempt to wash or vacuum these because they may fall apart. Instead, replace them when they are dirty.

Remember the vacuum. Do not forget to empty, clean, or replace vacuums bags and canisters as well. Like air filters, they rid the air of dirt and dust particles. However, if you continue to use them when they are full, they will only reintroduce the dirt back into the air.

Use plants as natural air filters. Indoor air is more toxic than the outdoor air. Consider introducing some of nature's filters to the interior of your home. Green houseplants, such as ferns or potted palms, are a great way to improve the indoor air quality at your residence. Be sure to research the plants you are bringing in. Some plants are poisonous and are hazardous if accidentally ingested by children or pets. There are a few plants that the

EPA cautions about using indoors if they are in reach of small children and animals: They are:

- **Mums** — leaves and stalks are poisonous
- **Common English ivy** — leaves are poisonous
- **Dumbcane, giant dumbcane, spotted dumbcane** — all parts are poisonous

Be sure to care for plants properly: Do not overwater them, as they can develop mold, and be sure to clip off any dead leaves and stems to keep the plant healthy. If your plant leaves get dusty, gently rub olive oil on them. It makes the plant look nice, and it is completely safe.

Consider other things you can grow that will help you around the house. Herbs are easy to grow and do not require a lot of space. You can start your own herb garden on your windowsill. It saves money and provides you with organically grown spices. They also make great gifts, and can be used in many of the cleaning supply recipes listed in Chapter 5. If you have a green thumb and space to work with, consider growing other produce you can use as well.

Freshen Air Naturally

We are accustomed to strong smells. Scents such as bleach and ammonia signify "clean." Likewise, we use numerous other artificial chemicals to make the house smell "cleaner" and more inviting. But a recent study showed that individuals who used air freshener sprays four times a week or more had twice as many incidences of physician-diagnosed asthma. Additionally, the National Resources Defense Council (NRDC) released a statement in 2007 stating that many commonly used air fresheners contained chemicals proved to affect normal hormonal and reproductive functions.

Instead of spraying chemicals, consider some of these alternatives to enhance the smell of your home:

- **Consider baking**. Home-baked goods smell great. Realtors often use this tactic when they are setting up an open house. Home-baked items such as breads, cookies, cakes, brownies, or pies make the house smell wonderful.

- **Boil spices that you like**. If you do not want baked goods around the house, you can achieve a similar affect by using some of the same ingredients. Any spice that appeals to you can be boiled. Cinnamon and nutmeg work particularly well, but any spice will work. You can also boil fruit peels, such as lemon and orange rinds, for a fresh, clean smell.

- **Dip cotton balls into pure extracts**. Pure extracts, such as vanilla and peppermint in small quantities, provide baked goods with tremendous flavors. Their smells are strong as well. You can pour a small amount of your favorite extracts into a bowl and place it on the kitchen counter to help eliminate cooking odors. As an alternative, you can dip a cotton ball into a small amount of your favorite extract and place it in a jar with a vented lid. This will create long-lasting fragrance in the room.

- **Use essential oils**. In addition to pure extracts, essential oils make nice air fresheners. A little bit of essential oil can make a big difference. Make your own countertop air freshener by placing some essential oil on a cotton ball and putting it in a clean, recycled glass jar. Use a knife to put slits or holes in the lid. You can purchase small containers of essential oils at drugstores, health food stores, or online stores.

CASE STUDY: IMPROVING INDOOR AIR QUALITY WITH HOUSEPLANTS

Bill Wolverton, Ph.D.
Wolverton Environmental Services, Inc
www.wolvertonenvironmental.com

Dr. Wolverton is a retired NASA research scientist and President of Wolverton Environmental Services, Inc. Wolverton, who has a Ph.D. in environmental engineering, was employed with the U.S. government for more than 30 years — many of which were with NASA as a research scientist. His NASA research concerned the development of a closed ecological life support system for future permanent space habitats. After retiring from NASA, he directed his research with plants and microorganisms toward solving earthly environmental pollution problems, such as improving indoor air quality, treating domestic sewage and industrial wastewater, and treating and recycling water in intensive fish culture. He published several books on the subject and has a new one due out by the end of 2009, titled Plants: How They Contribute to Human Health and Well-Being *(Roli Books).*

During the Skylab III mission, NASA discovered 107 volatile organic chemicals (VOCs) emitting from synthetic materials inside the spacecraft. NASA then realized that indoor air pollution in a tightly sealed structure could present health-related problems.

In 1980, at the John C. Stennis Space Center in Mississippi, my colleagues and I first discovered that plants could eliminate VOCs from sealed test chambers. Following many repetitive tests, the findings were first published in 1984. To further investigate these findings, NASA had created a "Biohome" that was constructed of all synthetic materials. Its exterior consisted of molded plastic panels and used thick fiberglass insulation to make it super energy-efficient.

The Biohome had a total interior space of approximately 640 square feet and was fully equipped to serve as a one-person habitat. Because the building materials and interior furnishings consisted of primarily synthetic products, it was assumed that the outgassing of fumes from these products would lead to serious indoor air-quality problems. Indeed, upon entering the Biohome, most people began to experience burning eyes and throats, respiratory problems, and other symptoms commonly associated with "sick building syndrome." As is usually the case, the symptoms disappeared after leaving the building.

The ability of plants to remove airborne VOCs was tested by placing plants around the living quarters. Scientists also placed inside one small, experimental, fan-assisted planter containing a plant growing in a mixture of soil and activated carbon.

CASE STUDY: IMPROVING INDOOR AIR QUALITY WITH HOUSEPLANTS

Prior testing had shown that this prototype had the VOC removal ability of 15 regularly potted plants. After several days, sophisticated chemical analyses showed that almost all VOCs were removed. Most importantly, persons entering the Biohome no longer complained of irritating symptoms.

A student then lived in the Biohome for one summer and experienced no discomfort. The Biohome served as the first "real world" test, proving the ability of houseplants to improve indoor air quality.

In 1989, EPA reported to the U.S. Congress that they had detected more than 900 VOCs in the air of public buildings. After many years of research, we now have a better understanding of just how important it is for us humans to remain in close contact with nature. Research has shown that interior plants remove harmful airborne toxins; add much-needed moisture to the often dry indoor environment; release beneficial negative ions; and provide a connection to nature that promotes human health and well-being.

Based on my research, I recommend the following plants for improving the indoor air quality in a residential setting:

- Lady palm
- Areca palm
- Rubber plant
- Peace lily
- Golden pothos

Lighting

After addressing the indoor air quality, you may want to review the lighting in and around your home. Lighting is an easy place to make eco-friendly changes. By making small changes in the types of lighting you use and how you use it, you can be eco-friendly and fiscally responsible, as well.

The Energy Independence and Security Act of 2007

According to the U.S. Energy Independence and Security Act of 2007, otherwise known as the "Energy Bill," current, traditional incandescent lighting sources will eventually be phased out. The changes are not yet mandated in the United States. Currently, this is regulated on a state-by-state basis. California is the first in the United States to consider enforcing these regulations. In California, the plan is to phase out incandescent lighting by 2018.

By January 2012, the traditional 100-watt bulb will be eliminated in the European Union. The plan is to gradually eliminate incandescent lighting for sources that are up to 70 percent more efficient. As of September 1, 2009, 100-watt incandescent bulbs were no longer available in shops in 27 countries in Europe. These types of bulbs use up to 80 percent more electricity than the newer compact fluorescent versions.

Use as necessary

Remember the three Rs of the environmental movement: "reduce, reuse, and recycle." Using less lighting and other forms of electricity is an easy place to reduce. Everyone can reduce waste by cutting back consumption a little bit every day by not leaving lights and other appliances on when they are not in use.

- Open your curtains during daylight hours to reduce the need for inside lighting.

- Turn lights off when leaving a room, unless you will be in and out of the area repeatedly over a brief amount of time. Turning the light on and off frequently can actually use more energy.

- Have kids spend more time outside and less time in front of the television or computer.

- Use candles at dinner.

Go fluorescent

Compact fluorescent light bulbs, also known as CFLs, use 25 percent less energy and heat than standard incandescent light bulbs. Additionally, they are made to last up to ten times longer. Therefore, they save energy and money in the long run. You can now replace all standard lighting fixtures with CFL options in your home. As your current light fixtures burn out, replace them one by one with CFLs. According to the EPA's Energy Star program, about 20 percent of in-home energy usage is lighting. The organization urges people to start changing to CFL lighting to promote energy saving across the country. According to the EPA, if every home in the United States replaced even one traditional bulb with a CFL, it could save enough energy in a single year to light 300,000 homes. The most-used lights in the home are generally in the kitchen, the family room, and on the home's exterior. When purchasing any lighting that boasts energy efficiency, make sure it has the Energy Star logo.

Try light-emitting diodes

Light emitting diodes, or LED, use much less energy and last much longer — up to 100,000 hours. LEDs have been used for years in electronics, flashlights, and Christmas lights. Many companies are experimenting in ways to incorporate them in other forms of lighting. Philips Lighting has recently come up with a variety of products such as street lamps, retrofit bulbs, and recessed lighting. This kind of lighting is still expensive but given the product lifespan, which is a good investment. Another advantage is the fact that LEDs do not contain mercury. If you go camping or want an alternative light source for power outages at home, consider purchasing an LED hand-crank lantern. One turn of the handle provides 20 minutes of light with no electricity or batteries necessary.

Add energy-saving devices

Even a small change can make a big difference. If you have electric outdoor lighting, reduce use by setting it on a timer or motion detector. The detectors use photo sensors and come on when humans come close to the property, and the timer also limits use. There is no need to have full-fledged lighting for 12 hours. Remember to adjust it as necessary during the change of seasons and daylight saving time. In addition to timers, consider adding dimmer switches. These allow control over the amount of light used in a room. It increases energy efficiency by reducing wasted light and allowing you to use only what you need at a given time. You can also add switches that turn off multiple lights at one time.

Use solar power

Outdoor lighting provides safety and security in addition to looking nice around your property. There are a number of solar options available in garden and walkway lighting. If you are building or upgrading your home, there are many additional options for adding solar panels and skylights.

Switch to green power

According to U.S. Department of Energy, more than half of the consumers in the United States now have the option to have their electricity supplied by something known as "green power." The Green Power Network provides electricity that is powered at least in some part by renewable energy resources. These include solar, wind, geothermal, and hydropower. Green power is currently run on a state-by-state basis. To find out if this is an option in your area, you can contact your electric company, or check the U.S. Department of Energy Web site at **http://apps3.eere.energy.gov/green-power/markets/index.shtml**.

Clean your light fixtures

Like everything else inside your home, light fixtures acquire dust. Keeping them clean improves their efficiency, so do not neglect them during regular surface cleaning. To clean light bulb fixtures, wait until they are completely cool, and wipe with a clean rag or microfiber cloth that is lint-free. Outdoor lighting sources may be wiped down first with a damp cloth, followed by a dry cloth. Depending on the type of lighting, you may also need to empty the fixture to remove dead insects. It is common to find an accumulation of dead insects in lighting fixtures. Rather than dump them in the trash, you can empty the contents into your garden or compost pile.

CASE STUDY: GENERAL CONTRACTOR DISCUSSES ENERGY-EFFICIENT, ECO-FRIENDLY HOME UPGRADES

Tom Brunner
General Contractor
Owner TDB Enterprises LLC
Shiremanstown, PA

Tom Brunner owns and operates TDB Enterprises, LLC. He has owned his own home-remodeling and general contracting business for eight years. During that time, he has observed an increased demand for environmentally friendly products in and around the home. These are some simple eco-friendly and energy-efficient changes he suggests to his customers.

As a general contractor, I frequently get requests to install eco-friendly materials and energy-saving devices. Many are worth the time and money in the long run. For example, I am a proponent of composite decking when people ask me to build them a deck. It is more expensive, but it will not crack, rot, or splinter like

CASE STUDY: GENERAL CONTRACTOR DISCUSSES ENERGY-EFFICIENT, ECO-FRIENDLY HOME UPGRADES

traditional wood. It is easier to clean and does not require any special products, such as stains or other chemicals.

When I install outdoor lighting for decks, porches, or landscapes, I suggest the customer add low-voltage outdoor lighting with timers, or dusk-to-dawn photo cell switches. These devices are somewhat safer and more energy-efficient. These are also a good replacement for the regular manual on/off switches. Additionally, I suggest installing solar fixtures as an eco-friendly money saver that completely eliminates electrical needs.

In regard to interior lighting fixtures, I sometimes recommend CFLs (compact fluorescent light bulbs) for new installs. They just make sense in the long run. Why change a bulb every couple of months if you do not have to? If you are installing new fixtures, make sure you use the right type of bulb if you want to add dimmer switches. Check the wattage requirements and labels to make sure you are using a "dimmable CFL bulb." I have had multiple people call me with blown circuits because they did not check this before trying to install it themselves.

I also highly recommend putting a timer on exhaust fans, particularly in bathrooms. It is a good energy saver because people tend to leave them on indefinitely. Exhaust fans are important because they help prevent mold growth, but people do forget and leave them on all day. Leaving these devices on all day is a waste of energy. Instead, I suggest adding a timer. Again, there is a cost in the beginning, but in the end, it is a worthwhile return for a small monetary investment.

New products are constantly created. Home improvement stores and the Internet are good sources of information on the newest eco-friendly products on the market.

Insects and Other Uninvited Indoor Pests

Not only do insects gather in your light fixtures, but they seep into virtually all areas of your home. Even the most vigilant house cleaners must deal with insects at least occasionally. In addition to insects, some homeowners must also combat various rodents such as mice. There are numerous commercial products available for dealing with pest control. Common pesticides, as they are called, are readily available in grocery stores, hardware stores, garden supply stores, and discount chain stores. It seems simple enough, right? They are easy to find, easy to use, and are relatively afford-able. But the problem is these products are developed to eradicate pests. They are intended to be toxic, thereby killing the pests. By introducing these substances in and around your home, you dramatically increase the amount of toxins you are exposed to. If you use a professional pesticide company, the amount of toxins increases even more.

Commercially sprayed pesticides and pesticide bombs contaminate every-thing in the home. They linger on flooring and walls and become imbed-ded in carpeting and other household furnishings. The chemicals remain for several weeks afterward.

An August 2009 issue of *Science Daily* describes a study done at George-town University's Lombardi Comprehensive Cancer Center. The study suggests there may be a possible link between the use of pesticides and certain types of childhood cancer. The research revealed increased levels of common household pesticides present in the urine samples of children with acute lymphoblastic leukemia. The journal stated that although the study's results should not be considered definitive, they certainly warranted further research. Another study done in Berkeley, California, showed infer-tility in males working for commercial pesticide companies. The increased exposure to pesticides seemed to create lingering effects.

According to the EPA, there are more than 1,055 active ingredients reg-istered as pesticides. These ingredients are formulated into thousands of pesticide products and are currently are available in the marketplace. Since pesticides are toxic by nature, exposure creates many potential health threats. Some are mild; others are more severe. Health risks from pesticide exposure include:

- Rash and other skin irritation
- Eye irritation
- Nervous system damage
- Hormonal disruption
- Reproductive problems
- Tumors
- Cancer

If you currently use a commercial pesticide, or pesticide service, make sure to review the most up-to-date information provided by the EPA. They publish a pamphlet on using pesticides. It is available online at **www.epa. gov/oppfead1/Publications/Cit_Guide/citguide.pdf**.

What is the Alternative?

Prevention

Before using pesticides, you should take steps to avoid the need for them in the first place. Here is a list of simple preventative measures:

- Clean up food and beverage spills immediately.

- Do not leave food out.

- Keep all food items stored in tightly sealed containers if they are not in the refrigerator or freezer. Items that attract bugs, such as different types of sugars, may be stored in the refrigerator.

- Be vigilant in keeping kitchen surfaces clean and crumb-free. Do not forget neglected crumb collectors, such as toasters and toaster ovens.

- Repair screens.

- Seal cracks around windows and foundations.

- Eliminate clutter, where pests sometimes make their homes.

- Keep household areas as dry and dust-free as possible.

- Do not forget to vacuum upholstery and under cushions, where crumbs sometimes linger.

Coexistence

After taking reasonable preventative measures, consider which pests you can coexist with. Certain pests, such as rodents, pose health risks. Others, such as spiders, are mildly annoying but help eliminate other insects.

Use Non-Toxic Ingredients as Natural Repellents

There are numerous recipes for homemade pest repellents. They can be very effective at deterring pests from entering your home. *For basic formulas, refer to Chapter 5.* In addition to creating homemade pest repellents out of multiple ingredients, you can use a few simple substances alone to deter pests.

Oil

Insects do not like oil. In fact, it smothers them. Rub olive oil or other vegetable oil on your indoor plant leaves. This gets rid of dust, makes your plants look shiny and clean, and deters insects.

Vinegar

Insects, ants in particular, do not like the strong smell of vinegar. Cleaning your kitchen counters, floors, and refrigerator with vinegar deters them from invading. In addition to cleaning with vinegar, you can keep ants away by spraying vinegar along doorways, windowsills, countertops, crevices, under cabinets, and anywhere else that ants are likely to appear. If you find an ant trail or path repeatedly used by ants, clean the area with vinegar.

Peppermint extract

Mice and other rodents do not like the strong smell of pure mint. Soak cotton balls in peppermint extract and place them strategically around the house. To ensure the safety of small children and animals, place the cotton balls in sealed glass jars with ventilated lids. If your walls have small holes and cracks and you cannot effectively seal them, consider stuffing them with steel wool pads, such as those sold as kitchen scrubbers.

Baking soda

Baking soda may be used as productive insect repellent when sprinkled near cracks and crevices where pests might enter the home. It can safely be sprinkled all around your home's foundation. The substance irritates insects' exoskeletons, which contain chitin. They will avoid going near it.

Integrated Pest Management (IPM)

The EPA states that the need for environmentally friendly products includes the handling of insects and other pests as well. The current approach is called Integrated Pest Management (IPM). According to the EPA, IPM is an effective and environmentally sensitive approach to pest management that relies on a combination of common-sense practices. The programs utilize pest-specific information, such as their life cycles and their means of interacting with the environment. The information is considered and combined with the least hazardous means of dealing with the pests in question. IPM applies to agricultural and non-agricultural settings. The EPA recommends using these principles and practices in the home, garden, and the workplace. The practices are based on a four-tier approach. The steps include:

1. **Setting action thresholds — Determining the need for action**

   Before taking any action in regard to pest control, IPM suggests setting guidelines, called an "action threshold." This is the point at which pest conditions actually require action. A pest sighting does not necessarily mean control is needed; the number of pests and potential threats they pose should be taken into consideration.

2. **Monitoring and identifying pests — Deciding on an appropriate course of action, if any**

   According to the EPA, not all pests require control. Many organisms are harmless, and some are even beneficial. This approach monitors pests in order to make appropriate control decisions that take the action thresholds into account.

3. **Prevention — Managing areas in a manner that would eliminate the need for control**

   The IPM approach suggests working to manage indoor and outdoor areas in a way that prevents pests from becoming a threat in the first place.

4. **Control — Choosing the least risky practice to handle the problem**

   The prior steps indicate whether pest control is necessary. Control is based on the most cost-effective, least risky manner of handling or controlling the threats of the pest in question.

Chapter 8

Confronting the Kitchen

"The best way to get rid of kitchen odors: Eat out."

— Phyllis Diller, American comedienne

What to Avoid and Why

The information below depicts general types of cleaning products used in the kitchen. Different brands of products have different formulas. It includes a general list of harmful side effects that may possibly be produced from some chemicals used in these types of products. These side effects can occur even when properly using the products. This is because you breathe in the fumes from several chemicals. Always review all labels on your products before using them, and pay attention to any health-related side effects you may incur while using these or any other cleaning products.

Sink detergents

- **Diethanolamine (DEA)** — upper respiratory problems; skin irritation

- **Sodium hydroxide (also called caustic soda or lye)** — eye and skin irritation, ranging from mild to severe; gastrointestinal problems

- **Sodium laureth sulfate (or sodium lauryl ether sulfate)** — eye and skin irritation; potential brain, liver, heart, and tissue damage

Dishwasher detergents

- **Sodium hydroxide (also called caustic soda or lye)** — eye and skin irritation, ranging from mild to severe; gastrointestinal problems

- **Hydrogen chloride** — respiratory and digestive irritation; in severe cases, chemical burns and pulmonary edema

- **Hypochlorite** — eye, skin, and respiratory irritation; tissue damage

Oven cleaners

- **Sodium hydroxide** — eye and skin irritation; burning; upper respiratory obstruction; loss of measurable pulse; abdominal pain and vomiting; potential hemorrhaging

All-purpose cleaners

- **Ammonia** — eye, mucus membrane, and skin irritation; coughing; burns; asthma; lung damage

- **Bleach** — lung damage; asthma

- **2-butoxyethanol and 2-butoxyethanol acetate** — eye, mouth, and nose irritation; headaches; vomiting

- **Calcium hypochlorite** — nasal irritation; sore throat; eye and skin irritation; coughing

- **Sodium hypochlorite** — nasal irritation; sore throat; eye and skin irritation; coughing

Quick Kitchen Cleaning Tips

The kitchen is typically the center of the home. It is the primary source of food storage, as well as dinnerware, glasses, and utensils. It is where you prepare the majority of your meals, and many people store cleaning supplies under the sink or in other cabinets. Considering that it is the source of food and beverages you put in your mouth, it is the worst possible place to have toxic chemicals. If you need to keep toxic products in your home, consider the garage, basement, closet, or other storage area — away from the food supplies.

The kitchen possesses many potential germs and bacteria if food is not properly handled. However, spraying strong chemicals on counters that touch food items, plates, and utensils is not the answer. Instead, pull out two non-toxic items you have in your kitchen cabinets: vinegar and baking soda. These two substances are used in cooking, and are non-toxic and completely safe. Not only that, but they clean very well and can be used on virtually any surface. In addition to cleaning, both will eliminate unpleasant kitchen odors in refrigerators, the trash can, and garbage disposal.

All About Vinegar

If you had to get rid of every household-cleaning product you owned and could only use one eco-friendly substance to clean with, vinegar would be the one to choose. It is an extremely versatile substance. In addition to its usefulness in cooking, it can be used in home medical treatments, gardening, and household cleaning.

Vinegar is a liquid that results from fermentation. It has been around for more than 1,000 years. The word is derived from the French term "vin aigre," which literally translates into "sour wine." There are many types of vinegar, including white, apple cider, balsamic, and rice. The flavors depend on the ingredients used in the fermentation process.

Vinegar is a form of acetic acid, which makes it an excellent cleaning product, particularly for glass. Over the years, people began using it for virtually all of their cleaning needs. The only difference is the amount of water added to the substance to clean certain specific surfaces. For the cleaning purposes in this book, the term always denotes distilled white vinegar. Subsequently, in all of the applications described, the least expensive form of distilled white vinegar will work.

What About Baking Soda?

If you were to add only one other non-toxic substance to your simplified cleaning arsenal, it should be baking soda. What exactly is baking soda, anyway? It is a chemical salt byproduct otherwise known as bicarbonate of soda. It is an alkaline substance, thus providing it with the ability to neutralize acids, break down stains, and stabilize pH levels. These qualities make it great for household cleaning and laundering.

Some people confuse baking soda with baking powder; however, they are two different substances. Baking soda is pure bicarbonate of soda. Baking powder is basically mixture of agents — generally, baking soda, cream of tartar powder, and starch.

Like vinegar, baking soda has many uses other than for cooking. For example, it may be used to extinguish small grease fires in the kitchen. It can also serve as an abrasive cleaning agent, insect repellent, laundry supplement, and deodorizer.

Keeping it Clean

Kitchens are one of the toughest rooms in the house to get and keep clean. This is a high-traffic area. People are in and out of the kitchen several times a day, bringing germs and other bacteria. In addition to germs, other common household pests are also drawn to the kitchen for food. Some food items may carry germs and pests in or on them when they are brought into the home. Food and drinks are also taken out for preparation and eating multiple times during the course of a single day. This creates a greater possibility of exposure to bacteria. Additionally, not everyone is neat. Individuals may leave a trail of crumbs or a small spill behind them without totally cleaning it up.

This is one room that really requires vigilance. Keeping the countertops and appliances clean not only make it look nicer, but it can greatly decrease the number of viruses and stomach ailments you and your family members might suffer from.

The Counters Come First

Kitchen counters require constant cleaning. Clean them off after every meal, and make sure spills and crumbs are immediately removed. That sounds obvious, but anyone with children knows that is not always the case. In addition to wiping them down on a regular basis, you should deep-clean them once a week.

- First, remove everything on top of the counters.

- Look for crumbs under appliances. Sweep them into your hands and put them in the sink.

- Fill a clean, empty spray bottle with equal parts vinegar and warm tap water. If you are sensitive to the vinegar smell, you can add a little bit of lemon juice or a couple of drops of essential oil. Remember, pests do not like the strong smell of vinegar, so if you can stand it, use it without adding a fragrance. It is worth it to make it unpleasant for insects — and the smell dissipates quickly.

- Spray vinegar solution on counters and splash guards. Wipe down the entire area with a soft cloth.

- If caked-on, hard-to-remove sticky spots or stains remain, use baking soda paste to remove them. You can make the paste by combining equal parts of baking soda and water, and stirring until the mixture becomes a creamy, paste-like substance. For difficult stains, cover the area with the baking soda paste and let it sit for 10 to 15 minutes. After that, take a soft cloth and rub the mixture over the stain using a slow, circular motion until it goes away.

As an alternative to baking soda paste, you can rub half a lemon over the stain. *You can also try one of the recipes for an all-purpose cleaning solution included in Chapter 5. If you have certain countertop surfaces that require special handling, refer to Chapter 14 for additional information.*

Small Appliances

Before putting items back on top of your countertops, wipe them down. Otherwise, you are reintroducing dirt to the area you just cleaned. Smaller items, such as knife blocks, spoon rests, and utensil holders, can be wiped down with a soft cloth that has been sprayed with the vinegar solution. Be sure to pay particular attention to the bottoms of these items before return-ing them to the clean counter.

If you keep small appliances — such as a toaster, blender, can opener, or coffee pot — on top of the counter, dump any crumb remnants over the sink. Then check the appliances inside and out for lingering dirt. If the appliances are not used frequently, they can become dirty by harboring normal household dust. In addition, you should carefully run the soft cloth along the entire plug to keep it clean as well. Do not introduce wetness to the plug head that goes into the socket. Along those lines, it is unnecessary to plug items in that are not being used. It is more energy-efficient and eco-friendly to plug them in only as you use them, since they usually draw power if they are plugged in, even if they are not in use.

Microwave ovens

If you own a microwave oven, you probably use it a lot. The more it gets used, the more it needs to be cleaned. Use the vinegar and water solution to clean the microwave inside and out. If it is a freestanding model that is not attached to the wall or a cabinet, be sure to lift it up and clean it under-neath. Wipe down the back and along the plug cord as well.

If the microwave is covered with food splatters or other dried-up food rem-nants on the inside, you can use several methods to soften and release the food particles. They all involve getting the microwave hot to loosen the dirt. Here are a few suggestions.

1. Mix 1 cup of water with ½-cup vinegar in a microwave safe bowl. Place the bowl in the center of the microwave and turn it on high until the liquid boils. Carefully take the hot bowl out of the micro-wave with a potholder and place it in the kitchen sink. The con-densation from the liquid loosens baked-on food particles, making

them easy to clean. Take a soft cloth and wipe down the softened food mess from top to bottom. Do not forget to wipe down the inside of the microwave door as well. Not only does this solution clean up splattered food messes, it also eliminates lingering odors from the microwave. When the vinegar solution in the bowl is cooled off, you can use a funnel to pour it in the spray bottle with the rest of your solution for other kitchen-cleaning jobs.

2. If you do not have any vinegar, or do not like the smell, you can accomplish the same goal by using a baking-soda-water solution. Mix 2 tsp. baking soda with ½-cup of warm water in a microwave safe bowl. Stir until the baking soda is thoroughly mixed in the water. Place the bowl in the center of the oven and turn it on high for two minutes. Carefully take the bowl out and put it aside. Wipe down the interior of the microwave with a soft cloth. Do not waste the remaining baking soda solution. Leave the rest of it on the counter to use for other kitchen cleaning as you go.

3. If you prefer the scent of lemons and happen to have a real lemon in the refrigerator, you can use it to clean the microwave as well. Cut a lemon in half and place half of the lemon in a microwave-safe container. Cover the lemon with 2 cups of cold tap water and place it in the center of your microwave. Turn the oven on high and set the timer for two minutes. Use a soft cloth to wipe down the oven's interior. Place the bowl of lemon water on the kitchen counter. It will act as a natural air freshener.

If you still have some lingering food remnants or grease in the crevices after you have wiped it down, you can use a baking soda paste, made from equal parts of baking soda and water. Dip a toothbrush in the paste and use it to scrub the crevices. Wipe down the remains with a damp, soft cloth. A toothbrush is an excellent tool for cleaning small, hard-to-reach areas of the house. You can buy an inexpensive version and keep it with your cleaning supplies. If you choose to use one that has been previously used, run it through the dishwasher with the utensils to get rid of germs first.

When you are done wiping down the interior of the microwave, unplug it and pull it out. Take out the interior plate and rotation mechanism, and place them in the sink. Wipe down all four sides and the top and bottom with the vinegar and water cleaning solution. Make sure to wipe down the plug cord as well. Next, clean off the microwave plate and rotation ring using a clean cloth dipped in vinegar. Dry them both off and replace them in the appliance.

To keep the microwave clean on a daily basis, keep a soft cloth nearby. Every time you use the microwave, wet the cloth with tap water and run the cloth over the warm interior. That way, it will not get as dirty to begin with and will not require as much elbow grease to clean it.

Coffee makers

If you use your coffee maker daily, you have probably noticed that it can get build-up deposits on it. For daily cleaning, either place the empty pot on the top rack of the dishwasher or wash it by hand, depending on the manufacturer's instructions. The rest of the appliance can be wiped down with a damp cloth. Some coffee makers have removable filter holders. If your does, remove it and rinse it in the sink as well. Once a week, clean the coffee maker's interior:

- Pour 1 cup of vinegar in the water reservoir and fill it to the top with hot tap water.

- Turn coffee maker on and run it as if you were making coffee, but with just the vinegar-water solution.

- When the cycle finishes, pour hot vinegar solution in a container and set it aside.

- Run coffee maker again with plain tap water to remove remaining residue. This will make the coffee pot cleaner and make the coffee taste better as well.

For particularly tough coffee stains, fill the coffeepot with water and add about 3 tsp. of cream of tartar. Stir the cream of tartar until it is completely dissolved, and run water though the coffee maker. Use a coffee filter as if you were making pot of coffee. When pot is full, let the water cool. Scrub the pot with a soft cloth or sponge and rinse well. If any stains remain, rub table salt into the stain with the wet soft cloth.

For optimum eco-friendly cleaning practices, reuse all the water you have used to clean the coffee maker. Use the plain water to feed plants. The vinegar solution can be used to clean the garbage disposal or sink drain.

Tea kettles

Despite only being used to boil water, teakettles can get just as dirty as coffee pots. Both items suffer from lime deposits, which is essentially a build-up of minerals that come from using hard water. If you are not sure whether you have hard water in your residence, you can usually tell by adding a little bit of water to a bar of soap. If it lathers quickly and easily, you most likely have soft water. If you have to work at getting it to lather, you may have hard water. Additionally, if you have hard water, you will notice staining on your coffee makers, teakettle, dishwasher, and faucets. To clean the teakettle:

- Pour either ½-cup of lemon juice or ½-cup of vinegar in the bottom of the teakettle, and fill the remainder with warm tap water.

- Bring liquid to a boil. While it is still warm, but not too hot to touch, clean the outside to remove any build-up of grease and grime.

- Use a soft cloth dipped in vinegar.

- To ensure that the inside gets clean, set the full teakettle aside overnight. In the morning, dump the contents of teakettle in your garden.

- Fill the teakettle with warm water again and bring it to a boil. Once the water is cooled, use it for watering your plants or cleaning. After that, the teakettle is clean and ready to use again.

- Repeat this process as often as necessary. It depends on your frequency of teakettle use. If you use it daily, clean it out once a week. If not, clean it once or month.

If you have a constant problem with hard water build-up on coffee makers, teakettles and other similar devices, you may want to purchase an anti-lime disc at a kitchen shop. The disc remains in the kettle and keeps mineral deposits from forming in the first place.

Stovetops and Indoor Kitchen Grill Surfaces

The stovetops are another area requiring vigilance. They are essentially an extension of your countertops and should be cleaned any time you clean your counters. Stovetops and ovens need to remain clean, as unattended food spills could result in a kitchen fire. Additionally, you should wipe them down each time you cook. Keep your bottle of vinegar-water solution somewhere nearby. When the stovetop is still slightly warm, spray some solution on your cloth, and wipe off any food or grease residue. Resist the temptation to let any mess sit until after the meal is over. Spills and grease are easiest to clean when they first happen.

Flattop cooking elements

Different types of cooking surfaces require different types of care. A flat top stove is the easiest to care for because spills cannot drip below the surface.

- Clean a flattop surface with a vinegar-water solution. Wipe it daily as needed.

- If a pot boils over and creates a caked-on food mess, use a baking soda paste to clear the stain.

- After the cooking element has cooled, cover the stain with baking soda paste.

- Let it sit for about 20 minutes. After that, rub it gently with a soft cloth until the mess is gone.

- Follow by spraying area with vinegar to remove any lingering cloudy residue.

Certain flattop surfaces require special handling. If you have a brushed-chrome surface, be sure to rub the soft cloth with the grain. This will help you avoid visible streaking in the chrome. If you have a tempered-glass or porcelain surface, be careful to avoid using too much water, because the water can seep under the glass. In this case, spray the vinegar-water cleaning solution on the soft cloth, rather than spraying it directly on the surface. Additionally, porcelain surfaces may become discolored if a spill is highly acidic, such as a tomato sauce. If this occurs, immediately use a dry, soft cloth to wipe up the spill. A dampened cloth on a hot porcelain surface is discouraged, as it may result in cracking or chipping.

Traditional electric stovetop cooking elements

Traditional electric stoves have raised heating elements. If you possess this type of stove, you may occasionally have an issue with food dripping below the heating element into the drip pan. To clean the drip pans, make sure the stovetop is completely cool. Carefully lift the heating element by the ring and remove the drip pan. Depending on the amount of dirt, you can clean them any of the following ways:

- Spray each drip pan with vinegar-water solution and wipe clean with a soft dry cloth. Then replace drip pans under the cooking element.

- Scrub caked-on food messes with baking soda paste. Rinse with warm water and finish off the surface by spraying with vinegar solution and wiping dry before returning drip pans.

- Soak dirty drip pans in warm soapy water in the sink and rinse with clear warm water. Wipe dry with a clean dishcloth and replace drip pan under cooking element.

- Place drip pans in the dishwasher when you run it. If you do this every night, they may show signs of wear, but it is fine to do it occasionally if you have a particularly tough mess to clean up. Remove from dishwasher and dry with a towel to remove any water spots before replacing them under the cooking element.

- If all of these options fail to get them clean, it is safe to cover the drip pans with tin foil. After tightly wrapping the drip pans, replace them under the cooking element and they are ready to use.

While the drip pans are removed, spray the surrounding area with vinegar and water to clean any residue that may have slipped under the edges of the drip pan. If caked-on food exists, use a baking soda paste and rub it into the food stain until it loosens. Wipe clean and follow it with the vinegar solution.

Gas stove surfaces

Newer gas stoves have sealed stovetop burners that cannot be removed. This prevents spills from going below into the burner box. If food spills during cooking, turn off the burner and move the pan to another burner until you finish cooking. Be sure the burner is completely cooled before attempting to clean the surface.

Clean the area with a damp cloth. Dampen the cloth with warm water and squeeze out any excess. You do not want to get any water in the gas tube. Also, take care not to bump the gas ignition element. You do not want to damage it; if it gets bent or wet, it may not be able to light the burner. If one of the gas elements gets clogged with food debris, you can carefully clean it when the stove is off and completely cooled. It is best to use a straight pin or the end of a metal paper clip. They will not break off and get into the gas port. With the point of the pin, carefully clear the clogged area. If you do not have a straight pin or a paperclip, you can try to clear the debris by gently running a toothbrush head over the clogged surface until the debris is cleared.

Indoor grill cooking surfaces

If your kitchen includes a built-in grill-cooking surface, you can clean it by removing the different parts of the grill.

- Be sure the grill is off and cool before attempting to clean it.

- Carefully remove the grilling grates and drip pans. Depending on the size of the surface and the degree of dirt, it may be a messy job.

- Place the grill top and drip pans in the sink to clean it. If the grease is caked on, rub each grate with baking soda paste in an up-and-down motion, thoroughly coating each rod in the process.

- Let it sit coated in baking soda paste for 30 minutes. After letting it sit, use old, sturdy rags, such as ripped-up towels, to scrub the surface of the grill and the drip pans.

- Rub the baking soda mixture with the rags until the grease is loosened.

- Rinse the grates and drip pans with plain, hot tap water.

- Remove any remaining residue with vinegar and water.

- Dry with a clean cloth before replacing it on the cooking surface.

- Built-in grill tops also have collection jars for the grease. Scoop out the grease when it is cooled and solid. Put it in the trash. The collection jar can be washed in the sink or placed in the dishwasher.

Hooded vents

Regardless of the type of cooking surface you have, you most likely have a hooded vent hanging above it. These hooded vent systems become covered in greasy residue from cooking. The best way to clean is the vinegar-water solution. Spray it on and rub with a soft cloth. If you have a large amount of grease residue that is difficult to remove, you can use straight vinegar without water to clean it off. Vinegar is acidic and therefore an excellent degreasing agent. It also leaves surfaces clean and shiny. You can use pots and pans that match the size of the heating element on your cooking surface to reduce the potential for messy spills and over-boiling. It also helps in cooking foods more evenly and effectively, eliminating unnecessary burnt-on food to clean up from the bottom of the pan.

The Oven

A clean oven works more efficiently and smells better. If something spills and you do not clean it up, then the next time you turn on the oven, it will smell — or worse yet, cause a fire. If you are lucky enough to own a self-cleaning oven, your cleaning time will be lessened considerably. If something falls or spills during cooking, clean the oven as soon as you are done cooking. It will be easier to maintain.

Using the self-cleaning feature on your oven is much more eco-friendly than using commercial oven-cleaning products. Oven-cleaning products use strong chemicals that produce toxic fumes. In addition, running the self-cleaning feature costs less than a can of oven cleaner.

- To use the self-cleaning feature, follow the manufacturer's instructions. Generally, the process takes a couple of hours. If there is a lot of caked-on food, it may smell during the process. If possible, open nearby windows while the self-cleaning cycle is running.

- When the cycle is complete and the oven has cooled, take a damp, soft cloth and wipe away any residue.

If you do not have a self-cleaning oven, clean it while it is warm but not too hot. You do not want to be burned.

- Spray the interior of the oven with the vinegar and water solution and wipe it off with a soft, clean cloth.

- If you have difficult-to-clean grease and grime, use a baking soda paste to work through the dirt.

- Rub the paste on and let it sit for 30 minutes.

- Rub the remains off with a cloth and follow up with the vinegar and water solution.

Even if you do not have major spills in your oven, clean it once a month to get rid of grease build-up. Also, in addition to cleaning your stovetop cooking elements and the interior of your oven, you need clean the exterior surfaces and the knobs.

- Spray the vinegar-water solution on the inside and outside of the oven door to get it clean.

- Some knobs come off for easier cleaning. If yours come off, remove them and rinse carefully with warm, soapy water. Make sure they are completely dry before replacing them.

- If the knobs are not removable, use the corner of a soft cloth dipped in vinegar to clean behind the edges of the knob. This area can get particularly greasy.

- If you have a freestanding oven (one that is not in the wall), pull the unit out once a month to clean underneath it. This area can get very dirty. When the oven is pulled out, clean the floor and wipe down walls on either side of the oven.

Cookware

There are numerous types of cookware on the market. Each surface type has its own properties, and you should pay attention to the manuals that accompany them in the packaging. For example, many types of cookware are not dishwasher-safe. None of them need to be cleaned with harsh chemicals; after all, they are used to cook your food. But even surfaces that touch raw meat can be disinfected with vinegar, which is an edible substance. You may feel like you are getting things cleaner by using harsher chemicals, but you are actually exposing yourself to more toxic substances than the raw meat itself. Below is a list of various cookware types and some eco-friendly cleaning suggestions for each type.

- **Stainless steel**: Most stainless steel cookware is dishwasher-safe. Check the packaging to be sure. To avoid water spots, remove the pots from the dishwasher at the end of the wash cycle and wipe dry with a clean cloth. If staining occurs on the cookware's interior, fill the pot with one cup of vinegar and three cups of water, and bring it to a boil. After it boils, remove it from the heat until it cools. Rinse pot with warm tap water and wipe dry with a clean cloth. If the cookware surface looks dull or discolored, rub it all over gently with baking soda paste. Rinse with warm water and dry with a soft cloth.

- **Copper**: Wash copper pots and other cookware with warm soapy water in the sink and dry thoroughly with a dishcloth. Do not place them in the dishwasher; copper tarnishes easily when exposed to moist air. To clean off small tarnish spots, rub the spots with ketchup and let them air out for 15 to 20 minutes. Rub the ketchup off thoroughly with a clean, dry cloth. For more difficult spots, sprinkle the area with a pinch of regular table salt and rub one half of a lemon over the salted area. Rinse mixture off with clear, warm tap water and dry with a soft cloth.

- **Aluminum**: Wash aluminum cookware in warm soapy dishwater in the sink. Do not place in the dishwasher. If it gets stained or discolored, make a paste out of 1-½ Tbsp. of cream of tartar and 2 Tbsp. of vinegar. Mix the paste with 4 cups of warm water in the bottom of the stained pot and simmer until the stains disappear. Dump the contents of the pot into the sink. Rinse with warm tap water. Wipe dry with a clean cloth. If aluminum cookware is burnt or stained on the bottom, soak the pan in a dishpan with 4 cups of hot water and 4 cups of vinegar. Let the pan soak for several hours — or overnight, of the residue is particularly bad. Then, rinse with cool tap water and dry with a soft cloth.

- **Anodized aluminum**: Hard anodized cookware cannot be washed in the dishwasher. Clean it in a sink with warm, soapy water. For caked-on food debris, fill the interior of the pot with warm, soapy water and let it set for one hour. That will loosen any food residue. Finish cleaning as normal with warm, soapy water. Rinse with clear, warm tap water, and dry with a clean cloth.

- **Ceramic**: Ceramic cookware is dishwasher-safe. If there is cooked-on food debris in a ceramic pan, sit in the sink with 1 cup of vinegar and fill with hot tap water. Let it sit for one hour. This will loosen food particles. Drain the vinegar solution and wash the cookware by hand, or place it in the dishwasher.

- **Cast iron:** Cast-iron cookware cannot be cleaned in the dishwasher. After normal cooking, rinse with hot water and wipe with a clean cloth. You may use a very small amount of dish soap. Cast iron does not react well to chemicals, and using too much soap can ruin the pan's finish. If this occurs, re-season the pan by coating it lightly with 1 to 2 Tbsp. of vegetable oil and simmering it until it coats the pan. To remove food residue, sprinkle the pan with regular table salt and use a clean cloth to work it into the residue. Rinse with warm water and dry with a clean cloth.

- **Non-stick surface cookware:** Non-stick surface cookware cannot go in the dishwasher. Commercial dishwashing detergents use strong chemicals that will damage non-stick surfaces. Clean this type of cookware by hand with warm, soapy water. If the pot has stains, fill with warm tap water and 3 Tbsp. of vinegar, and bring it to a boil. Remove from heat and let it cool. Drain fluid and wipe clean with a soft, dry cloth. Be careful not to try to scratch off food residue with anything other than a nylon spatula or a soft cloth. Anything else could scratch the non-stick coating and ruin the pan.

- **Porcelain, enamel-coated cookware:** Porcelain enamel cookware is becoming increasingly popular. These items are generally made from cast iron or aluminum and coated with the porcelain finish. For best results, clean by hand in the sink with soapy, warm water. The dishwasher can damage the finish. For cooked-on food residue, allow the pan to soak in the sink filled with warm soapy water for one hour. Clean with a dishcloth or soft sponge. Do not use anything abrasive.

The Refrigerator

The refrigerator is easy to maintain if you clean it regularly. Make sure spills are wiped up immediately. Once a week, plan to deep-clean the interior. If you have a large family and a full refrigerator, this will take some time. If you live alone, this will be relatively easy.

- Empty the contents onto the counter one shelf at a time, beginning with the top shelf.

- Get out two large mixing bowls. Fill the first one with 4 cups of vinegar and 4 cups of warm tap water. Mix well with a large mixing spoon.

- Fill the second bowl with warm tap water and one squirt of sink dish detergent. Have two clean, soft cloths available. Place one cloth in each bowl of liquid. The refrigerator is a particularly good place to clean with vinegar, since it is an edible substance. After all, you do not want to spray toxic chemicals anywhere near the food you eat. In the refrigerator, the chemicals would linger and potentially poison the food.

- Dunk one soft, clean cloth in the vinegar mixture and squeeze out excess fluid. Use the cloth to wipe down the top shelf and the surrounding refrigerator walls and ceiling.

- Place it back in the bowl of vinegar mixture, unless it is very dirty.

- If it picked up excess dirt, rinse it in the sink under hot tap water until it is clean, then replace it in the vinegar cleaning solution bowl.

- Before replacing the items you removed from the top shelf, wipe them down with the other cloth from the dishwater solution. Pay particularly close attention to squirt bottle tops that may have dried gunk on them.

- Continue this process shelf by shelf until they are all clean. Do not forget to do the same with the refrigerator door.

When it comes to crisper drawers, it is best if you can completely remove them from the refrigerator to clean them.

- Empty the contents and clean the drawers over the kitchen sink.

- Dump out any crumbs and wipe down with the vinegar cleaning solution.

- Make sure to wipe the drawer interior with a dry cloth before returning it to the refrigerator. Wetness makes for a breeding ground of mold in a refrigerator.

- Check food and labels. Get rid of food that is old or expired to avoid the chance of mold growth or another form of bacteria, such as salmonella.

- Finally, place a small box of opened baking soda in the back on one of the shelves. This will absorb odors until you can clean the refrigerator the next time.

This is also a good time to ensure that your refrigerator and freezer are set at the proper settings. Over time, people or items in the refrigerator and freezer can bump the thermostat and inadvertently change the setting. If you are unsure, most appliances have a label inside to explain the best setting for maximum efficiency. Most refrigerators should be set between 37 and 40 degrees Fahrenheit. The freezer should be set between 0 and

5 degrees Fahrenheit. If they are at the wrong setting, it could affect the contents. It could cause condensation, molding, food damage, or freezer burn — all of which create a much bigger mess to clean up.

Freezers

After the refrigerator side is cleaned, start the same process on the freezer. If there are items that could get ruined by sitting them out on the counter, such as ice cream, consider placing them in a cooler. Two or three times a year, it is a good idea to defrost the freezer. If you have ice starting to accumulate on the shelves, it needs to be done. Otherwise, the freezer will not work well and take more electricity to run — and it may damage the food contained inside.

- To defrost the freezer, empty the contents of the appliance.

- Wrap newspaper around the items you remove and place them in coolers with tight lids.

- Turn the freezer off and unplug it. If your freezer is attached to the refrigerator, do not open the refrigerator door until you are done defrosting the freezer. This reduces the chance of food spoiling while the appliance is unplugged.

- Place large towels on the ground below the freezer and in the surrounding area to catch water from the melting ice.

- Use a pot of boiled water to speed up the process.

- Wear rubber gloves and dip a clean cloth into the boiling water, and squeeze it over the ice to accelerate the defrosting process.

If you have an automatic icemaker, this is a good time to clean that as well. Automatic ice dispensers can harbor germs, accumulate mildew, and take on flavors of freezer contents if they are not regularly cleaned.

- While the freezer is unplugged, locate the power bar above the icemaker storage tray.

- Remove the ice storage tray and clean it out in the sink with warm water and a small amount of sink dish detergent.

- Rinse with warm clear tap water and dry completely with a clean dishcloth.

- Wipe down the ice dispenser inside of the freezer with a clean cloth and vinegar cleaning solution. The vinegar will kill any lingering germs.

- Replace the dry ice storage tray and move the power bar back into place.

- Once all of the excess ice is gone from the freezer, throw the wet towels in the wash and finish the cleaning process.

- Wipe the shelves and interior door with the vinegar cleaning solution. Make sure you carefully dry each shelf and the door, so ice does not start to form again immediately.

- When it is clean, plug the unit in again and turn it back on. Replace the contents, reviewing the food and expiration dates as you go.

Once you have completed the cleaning process in the refrigerator and freezer, wipe down the outside. Pay particularly close attention to the seal around the door, the hinges, and the vent grates at the bottom. Once a month, pull the refrigerator out and clean underneath it as well. While it is pulled out, be sure to wipe down both sides of the exterior and clean off the unit's coils in the back. Clean coils help the appliance work more efficiently. Additionally, do not forget to clean off the top. Remove anything that is being stored on top of the appliance and wipe it down with the vinegar and water cleaning solution. The top of the refrigerator is an area that also gathers a lot of dust and grease over time.

The Dishwasher

There is an ongoing debate about the eco-friendliness of dishwashers. The latest studies indicate that dishwashers manufactured in the last ten years are very energy-efficient. If you only run the dishwasher when it is full and do not pre-wash the dishes before you place them in the dishwasher, the machine uses about 50 percent less electrical energy and about 80 percent less water. Therefore, using a dishwasher is often eco-friendly. If you only have a few dishes, however, wash them by hand in the sink.

Unlike sink dish detergent, many dishwasher detergents contain toxic chemicals. *See Chapter 5 for alternative recipes for dishwasher detergent.* Whether you choose to make your own homemade dishwasher detergent or use a commercial product, you need to clean out the machine at least once a month so that it continues to work properly. If your dishes are not getting totally clean, it may be because the dishwasher needs to be cleaned. Over time, bits of food particles and grease can build up in the appliance, just as it does in other appliances. Additionally, given the warm, moist environment, mold and mildew can form around the seal. To clean the inside of the dishwasher:

- Fill a small, dishwasher-safe cup with straight vinegar.

- Place the cup, opening side up, in the middle of the center of the top rack. Carefully close the door to the unit without placing any other dishes inside to be cleaned. Do not add dishwasher detergent.

- Run a full cycle on the hottest water setting. The vinegar will clean, freshen, and deodorize the inside of the dishwasher. It will also remove lingering soap scum that can leave a film on your glasses, dishware, and utensils. When the cycle is complete, open the door. There is no need to run the drying cycle.

- When the unit cools enough to touch the cup, remove it from the rack.

- Soak a clean cloth with warm tap water.

- Wipe down the interior of the appliance.

- Run the cloth along each fold of the door seal for best results. If there are dark spots on the seal, it may be the beginning of mold or mildew. Use your cleaning toothbrush dipped in vinegar and rub to remove black spots.

- If that does not work, try tea tree extract. It is found with the essential oils in health food stores. It is a natural non-toxic substance and very effective at removing molds. Do not use bleach or any product containing bleach — not only is it toxic, but it will break down the adhesion on the seal of your machine.

- Clean the exterior door of the appliance with the vinegar water solution.

- Finally, run a cloth soaked in vinegar and water cleaning solution along the grate at the bottom of the machine.

Garbage Disposal

If your sink has a garbage disposal, clean it once a week to remove greasy residue and lingering food odors. First, run the disposal while putting six ice cubes down the drain. The ice will help remove grease on the blades. Follow the ice with a full cup of straight white vinegar. Do not rinse. For best results, do not put anything else in the disposal for at least one hour.

Another grease solvent is regular table salt. Periodically, place equal parts of table salt and hot water in the disposal to keep the disposal grease-free and running efficiently.

Be very careful to follow the instructions on what you can put in the disposal. Do not dump items in the disposal that can expand by adding water. For example, mashed potato flakes in a drainpipe or garbage disposal will swell when water is added. This will essentially act like cement and clog the pipes. If you do get a clog in the garbage disposal, do not repeatedly run the disposal. This can damage the blades and burn out the motor. Additionally, never use a chemical drain-clearing product in the garbage disposal. They contain acid and can also cause damage. Instead, keep the disposal turned off, and call a plumber.

The Kitchen Sink

For regular kitchen sink drains, clean and deodorize weekly. First pour ½-cup of baking soda on top of the drain opening. Follow it with 1 cup of straight vinegar, and the solution will fizz. The chemical reaction will work at cleaning the germs out of the drain area and in the pipes below. Let the mixture sit for one hour. Then, flush with 3 cups of boiling tap water. Use the vinegar-water cleaning solution to clean the rest of the sink and faucets. This is safe for all sink types.

To remove hard water stains on the faucets, drape a vinegar-soaked soft cloth over the back of the faucet and let it sit for one hour. Afterward, wipe the stains clean with the cloth.

Do Not Forget the Cabinets

Kitchen cabinet doors and other exterior surfaces get covered in grease over time.

- A soft cloth soaked in warm water will remove most of the dirt.

- For stickier residue, spray the vinegar-water cleaning solution on a soft cloth and wipe off the grease.

- To clean the tops of the cabinets, remove items stored above and dust with a wet cloth.

- Wipe down any items before returning them to the cabinet tops as well.

- The biggest source of dirt and germs are the kitchen handles and drawer pulls. Wipe them daily with the vinegar-water cleaning solution.

- Do the same on the hinges.

- Once a week, pick a different cabinet to clean out.

The first should be under the kitchen sink. Pull everything out. If you have previously been storing your toxic cleaning supplies there, begin by getting rid of the products you can live without. Once you have pulled everything out, check for wetness. Make sure there are not any leaks from the sink or garbage disposal. If there are, make sure to repair them before putting anything back in the cabinet.

This cabinet in particular is at a great risk for mold and mildew. Also check for wetness caused from spilled products. If anything has spilled, sprinkle the surface with baking soda and let it soak overnight. Later, wipe the surface clean. The baking soda also absorbs the odor from whatever made the area wet. Before returning any products to the cabinet, wipe each item down. Consider storing your cleaning items together in a plastic bucket or bin. That way everything is together and ready to go when you need to clean. It also prevents the wood cabinets from getting damp and damaged from leaks and spills.

- Empty the contents and wipe the interior down with the vinegar-water cleaning solution.

- Make sure to clean the tops and bottoms of all shelving as well as the top, bottom, sides, and inside doors of the cabinet.

- Pay close attention to crevices where insect webs and egg nests can exist. Crumbs accumulate in all cabinets over time.

- By wiping the crumbs out and wiping the interior down with the vinegar-water solution, you decrease the chance of insects entering the area.

- As you empty the contents of the cabinets, review the items before you return them to the clean cabinets.

- Wipe everything down. Consolidate and organize similar items. Additionally, check expiration dates.

Clean out kitchen drawers in the same manner. Begin with the silverware drawer. Because it is opened several times a day, it tends to accumulate crumbs. If you have a removable silverware tray, remove it from the drawer.

Take out the silverware and clean the tray. Again, for best results, wipe all interiors with the vinegar-water solution and get all the crevices.

Cutting Boards

Cutting boards can harbor bacteria such as salmonella or E. coli. To be safe, use two separate cutting boards: one for meat and one for everything else. Some cutting boards can go in the dishwasher, depending on the material. To clean wooden cutting boards, stand board in the sink and pour vinegar on both sides. Let it sit for one hour. Rinse with warm water and dry with a soft cloth. Place upright in a drying rack until the wood has completely dried.

Baking soda and salt provide additional bacteria and odor resistance. Before using cutting board, rub with either baking soda or salt and a little bit of water. Brush off excess and wipe with a clean soft cloth. It is ready and safe to use.

If a plastic or glass cutting boards has strong odors from garlic, onions, or another strong smell, rub the item with a half of a lemon or rinse with straight vinegar. Here is another hint: Both vinegar and lemons will take the strong odors off hands, as well.

The Chef Burned Dinner — Now What?

If the burning results in a small grease fire, you can douse it by sprinkling on baking powder.

- After the fire is out, wait until the surface cools to remove the residue.

- Add a little water to the surface to make the baking soda into a paste.

- Rub the surface with a damp cloth until no residue remains.

- If the area is still cloudy, clean it off with vinegar and a clean cloth. Wipe until dry.

If the burnt meal is stuck to the cookware, sprinkle it with baking soda and cover with hot water. For best results, let the pan soak overnight. In the morning, rinse with warm water and clean with a soft cloth or sponge.

To get rid of the burnt-food smell and smokiness, first open the windows. Next, boil a pot filled with 3 cups of vinegar on the stove. Any type of vinegar will work. If there was a fire on the stove and it is unusable, you can place the 3 cups of vinegar in a bowl and put it on high in the microwave for two minutes. If that is not an option, leave a bowl of vinegar on the counter overnight. It will absorb the odors by morning.

The Kitchen Trash Can

The kitchen trash is another source of strong odors. Clean the outside of the trash can with the vinegar-water cleaning solution. Additionally, each time you take the bag out, sprinkle 1 tsp. of baking soda on the inside bottom of the can to deodorize it. Once a month, take the trash can outdoors and clean it thoroughly with warm soapy water. Rinse with a hose and wipe dry before bringing it back in the house.

Kitchen Food Scraps

One thing that can make the kitchen trash can smell foul is food waste. Instead of throwing food remains in the trash can with the rest of the garbage, consider these other eco-friendly ideas:

- If you have a garden, save the food remains for a compost pile. You can compost vegetable scraps, bread and other grains, pasta, coffee grounds, cereal, fruit peels, and egg shells. Animal byproducts, such as meat and dairy products, are not good for composting. *For more information on building a compost pile, refer to Chapter 16.*

- If you do not want to start a compost pile, place food scraps and other biodegradable trash items, such as grass clipping, raked leaves, and weeds, in a paper trash bags to put by the curb. Paper bags will biodegrade; plastic trash bags will not.

- Feed some safe food scraps to the dog. It is safe and healthy to mix vegetable scraps and other dog-friendly leftovers, such as meat scraps and rice, with the regular processed dog food.

The Kitchen Floor

When the rest of the kitchen is clean, it is time to tackle the floor. Sweep the kitchen floor every day. Every night, use a damp mop. Plain warm water is sufficient at this point. If there is a spill, address it immediately. If the spill is sticky, clean it with a wet cloth and the vinegar-water cleaning solution. This solution will also scuff marks and greasy residue. The best way to clean the kitchen floor is to get on your hands and knees once a week with soap and water and a sponge or rag. This allows you to get under cabinets and appliances to the areas that the mop does not reach. *To clean specific types of flooring, refer to Chapter 14.*

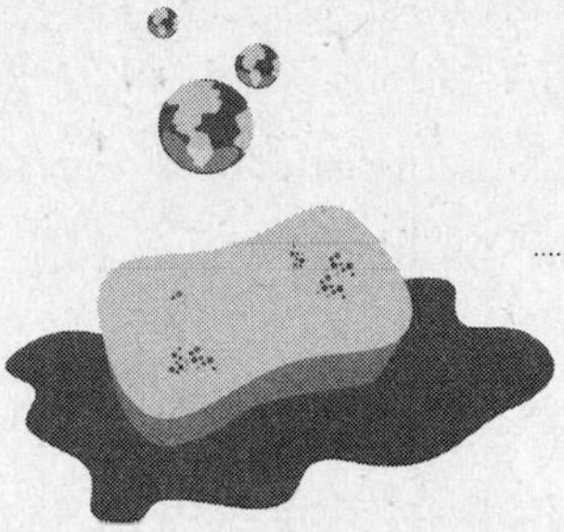

Chapter 9

Battling the Bathroom

"I don't know how you can clean someone else's toilet. I can barely touch my own."

— Francis McDormand, American actress

What to Avoid and Why

The following chart consists of general types of cleaning products used in the bathroom. Different brands of products have different formulas. This is a general list of harmful side effects stemming from the use of some of these types of products. Review all labels on your products before using them, and pay attention to any health-related side effects you may incur while using these or any other cleaning products.

Air-freshening sprays

- **Ethanol** — upper respiratory problems, eye irritation, headaches, and vomiting

- **Formaldehyde** — joint pain, depression, headaches, chest pains, ear infections, chronic fatigue, and dizziness

- **Naphthalene** — anemia, fatigue, nausea, vomiting, diarrhea, blood in urine, nasal and lung irritation, and skin discoloration

- **Phenol** — respiratory irritation, headaches, eye and skin irritation, liver damage, urine disturbances, and heartbeat irregularities

- **Xylene** — eye and skin irritation, nasal and throat problems, breathing difficulties, lung damage, memory difficulties, stomach upset, liver damage, and kidney damage

All-purpose cleaners

- **2-butoxyethanol and 2-butoxyethanol acetate** — eye, mouth, and nose irritation; headaches; and vomiting

- **Ammonia** — eye, mucus membrane, and skin irritation, coughing, burns, asthma, and lung damage

- **Bleach** — respiratory difficulties, headaches, skin burns, loss of consciousness, vomiting, lung damage, and asthma

- **Calcium hypochlorite** — nasal irritation, sore throat, eye and skin irritation, and coughing

- **Sodium hydroxide** — nasal irritation, sore throat, eye and skin irritation, coughing, respiratory problems, and gastrointestinal upset

Disinfectants

- **Chlorine** — breathing difficulties, eye and skin irritation, nasal irritation, lung damage, and coughing

- **Formaldehyde** — joint pain, depression, headaches, chest pains, ear infections, chronic fatigue, and dizziness

- **Phenol** — respiratory irritation, headaches, eye and skin irritation, liver damage, urine disturbances, and heartbeat irregularities

Drain cleansers/de-cloggers

- **Phosphoric acid** — eye and skin irritation, lung damage, and central nervous system problems

- **Sodium hydroxide** — nasal irritation, sore throat, eye and skin irritation, coughing, respiratory problems, and gastrointestinal upset

Mirror and glass cleaners

- **Ammonia** — eye and skin irritation, lung damage, nasal irritation, sore throat, coughing, burns, and gastrointestinal upset

- **Butyl Cellusolve** — eye, mouth, and nose irritation; headaches; and vomiting

- **Naphthalene** - anemia, fatigue, nausea, vomiting, diarrhea, blood in urine, nasal and lung irritation, and skin discoloration

Mold and mildew cleaners

- **Bleach** — eye and skin irritant, respiratory problems, asthma, and liver damage

- **Formaldehyde** — joint pain, depression, headaches, chest pains, ear infections, chronic fatigue, and dizziness

- **Phosphoric acid** — eye and skin irritation, lung damage, and central nervous system problems

Toilet bowl cleaners

- **Ammonia** — eye and skin irritation, lung damage, nasal irritation, sore throat, coughing, burns, and gastrointestinal upset

- **Bleach** — eye and skin irritant, respiratory problems, asthma, and liver damage

- **Caustic soda** — eye and skin irritation; gastrointestinal upset

- **Chlorine** — breathing difficulties, eye and skin irritation, nasal irritation, lung damage, and coughing

- **Hydrochloric acid** — eye and skin irritation, burns, fluid in the lungs, asthma, and skin discoloration

- **Naphthalene** — anemia, fatigue, nausea, vomiting, diarrhea, blood in urine, nasal irritation, lung damage, and skin discoloration

- **Phosphoric acid** — coughing, nose and throat irritation, stomach cramps, vomiting, burns, liver damage, and kidney damage

Tub and tile cleaners

- **Ammonia** — eye and skin irritation, lung damage, nasal irritation, sore throat, coughing, burns, and gastrointestinal upset

- **Bleach** — eye and skin irritation, respiratory problems, asthma, and liver damage

- **Chlorine** — breathing difficulties, eye and skin irritation, nasal irritation, lung damage, and coughing

General Quick Bathroom Cleaning Tips

The bathroom is the biggest source of germs in the home. Additionally, bathrooms generally contain trash cans and possible storage areas for cleaning products. All this combined in the smallest rooms of the house makes for potentially toxic circumstances.

Understandably, this is a room that requires serious cleaning. But it can be done without extreme chemicals with harmful side effects. As in the kitchen, vinegar and baking soda can service the majority of your cleaning needs. If you are consistent with your cleaning, you will never need to introduce toxic chemicals into this area.

As you begin your new eco-friendly cleaning methods, be sure not to mix the non-toxic substances with the old toxic substances. For example, the combination of acid substance with bleach can produce dangerous results. Therefore, never use bleach and vinegar together. It creates dangerously toxic fumes. Likewise, bleach should never be used near ammonia for the same reason.

Unlike the bathroom and other rooms, you will not clean using the top-down method; to best clean bathroom surfaces, many areas need to have cleaning agents sit for a while in order to clean most effectively. Start by applying the suggested cleaning agents to these areas, and work around them. By the time you are finished cleaning everything else, you can return to these areas and finish everything off. To simplify, do the following before beginning the rest of your bathroom-cleaning regimen:

- Flush the toilet. While the water is down, sprinkle 1 cup of baking soda along the water line of the toilet bowl. Next, pour 2 cups of vinegar over the same area. Let it stand.

- Sprinkle ½-cup of baking soda on top of the open sink drain and follow by pouring 1 cup of vinegar over top of it. Let it stand.

- Soak a soft, clean towel in vinegar. Place the towel around the bottom of your sink faucet and water knobs. Let the towel remain undisturbed for one hour.

- Sprinkle ½-cup of baking soda on top of the open tub drain and follow by pouring 1 cup of vinegar over top of it. Let it stand.

- Soak a soft, clean towel in vinegar. Place the towel over your tub faucet and water knobs. Let the towel remain undisturbed for one hour.

- Get a plastic bag and rubber band. Pour ½-cup of vinegar in the bag, and use a rubber band to tie the plastic bag tightly over the showerhead.

- Spray vinegar-water cleaning solution onto shower walls, shower doors, and tub basin. Let it stand without wiping.

- Take the shower curtain down and put in washing machine with hot water and 1 cup of vinegar. Let it soak in machine while cleaning the rest of the bathroom.

Once you have completed these preparation steps, continue on in the following manner.

Start with the Ceiling

After completing your simplified preparation steps, you can return to the top-down cleaning method. First, take the broom and sweep up along the ceiling edges and in the corners to ensure that no cobwebs or other small insects exist. Make sure the broom edge is clean before doing this, or you will add dirt there.

Next, address the middle of the ceiling. If it looks fine, run a soft cloth across it to dust it. If there are any spots on the ceiling, you may have a problem with mildew. Dark, warm, damp areas with insufficient circulation are prime areas for mildew growth. To prevent this from occurring, make sure you have a ceiling fan ventilation system for your bathrooms. Additionally, keep door and windows open in these areas as often as possible.

Attacking Mold and Mildew in the Bathroom

Mildew can cause health problems and damage to your home if not addressed immediately. As soon as you notice any spots on the ceiling, open up the area for air circulation. Open up doors and windows nearby, unless it is raining; adding more moisture to the air will defeat the purpose. It is important to attack the problem early and by non-toxic means. Many commercial mold- and mildew cleaners contain formaldehyde, which is a known carcinogen.

If you have a dehumidifier, place it in the room temporarily to extract excess moisture. If you do not have a dehumidifier, a floor fan will also work. Point the fan at the mildewing area. If there are multiple problem areas, you can rotate the fan as you clean. Make sure to keep any doors and windows open to minimize breathing in the mold and mildew. Mold and mildew can be very damaging to your lungs.

Next, pour 4 cups of straight vinegar in a small bucket and soak a cleaning brush in the vinegar for about 30 minutes while you are running the dehumidifier. Use the vinegar-soaked brush to scrub mold or mildew spots from the ceiling as soon as you see them form. It is easier to handle a small problem now than it is if you wait until it becomes a bigger problem.

Check the rest of the bathroom, paying close attention to the creases and crevices along the walls and floors and all areas of the shower and tub. If you find other mold or mildew spores, scrub there with the vinegar solution as well. To prevent the mold and mildew from occurring or reoccurring, do the following:

- Keep your bathrooms as dry as possible. When in use, use a good ventilation system.

- Wipe down your bathroom ceilings and walls weekly with vinegar. The acidic quality of vinegar helps prevent mold and mildew from occurring.

- For particularly stubborn areas, you can use common drugstore variety hydrogen peroxide to remove mold spores. It works well, and is more eco-friendly and less toxic than bleach.

- Make a preventative solution spray. Fill the spray bottle with hot tap water and five drops of tea tree essential oil. Tea tree oil is very good at combating mold. You can purchase it at most health food, beauty supply, or drug stores, or over the Internet. Spray the solution over damp areas once a week and wipe down with a soft, dry cloth.

What About the Walls?

To prevent mold and insects from gathering in your bathrooms, wipe down the walls once a week with a damp cloth covered in vinegar-water cleaning solution. If you have a window in the bathroom, be sure to open it to help dry and air things out. The vinegar smell will quickly dissipate.

Wall hangings may be problematic in bathrooms because of dust, hair, and dampness. Wreaths and dried-flower arrangements particularly do not hold up in this area. If you do have pictures or other wall hangings in the bathroom, be sure to take them down weekly and wipe them with vinegar-water cleaning solution as well. As you tend to the walls, be sure to carefully wipe light switches, doors, and doorknobs where fingerprints and germs gather daily.

Mirrors

After wiping down your ceiling and walls, it is time to clean the mirrors. There are many effective ways to clean the mirrors in your house. Again, vinegar is the best cleaning agent. It provides a clean, streak-free, germ-free shine to mirrors, windows, and all other surfaces you would otherwise clean with a glass-cleaning product.

- Use crumbled newspapers as an alternative to paper towels or cloth.

- Spray vinegar-water solution on the mirror surface.

- Rub in straight lines from top to bottom.

- Continue until the surface is completely clean. If slight streaking or smearing occurs, continue to rub in one direction until it fades.

According to Vince Caldor of the Office of Department of Energy's Office of Science Education, most newspapers now use water-based inks that are less inclined to smear. He suggests holding the piece of newspaper between your forefinger and thumb to test it out first. If you gently rub it between your fingers and the ink does not transfer to your hands, it is probably water-based ink. If it stains your hands, it may be oil-based and may create a problem for cleaning glass surfaces.

As an alternative to vinegar, consider mixing 2 cups of water and 1 cup of lemon juice in a spray bottle. Spray liquid on the mirror and wipe dry with a clean and dry, soft cloth. Since you want your mirrors to be streak-free, make sure to use a dry lint-free cloth. Lint and excess dampness can create streaking and smearing, which is why paper products are not the best to use to clean mirrors. If there is a window or any other glass surface in your bathroom, use the same method to clean those areas as well.

Do Not Forget the Cabinets

Bathroom medicine cabinets and other wood surfaces can get really dirty. High surfaces need to be checked for dust regularly. Hair can get all over from brushing and hair dryer use. Surfaces can get covered in greasy residue from personal grooming products, such as antiperspirants or hair sprays. Additionally, the warm, damp space may warp or cause mildew on wood surfaces.

For the most part, cabinets can be cleaned with a soft cloth soaked in warm water. Because the bathroom tends to be moisture-ridden, make sure the area is dry and well-ventilated as you are cleaning, and follow this method of cleaning by wiping excess moisture off with a dry cloth.

- Spray vinegar-water cleaning solution on a soft cloth and wipe greasy residue off cabinets.

- Clean the tops of the cabinets. Remove items stored on top of them and dust with a wet cloth. Wipe down any items before returning them to the cabinet tops as well. Again, follow this by wiping everything down with a dry cloth as well.

- Next, wipe any handles and drawer pulls with the vinegar-water cleaning solution. Do the same on the hinges. Open the doors and drawers, and wipe them down as well. Moisture and dirt can be trapped in these areas.

As you did the kitchen, check cabinets for toxic items. If you have previously been storing your toxic cleaning supplies or other items in this room, begin by getting rid of the products you can live without. Once you have pulled everything out, check for wetness. Make sure there are not any leaks from the sink. If there are, make sure to repair them before putting anything back in the cabinet.

The cabinet under the bathroom sink is a great risk for mold and mildew growth. Check for wetness caused from the sink and any spilled products. If anything has spilled, sprinkle the surface with baking soda and let it soak in overnight. Later, wipe the surface clean. The baking soda also absorbs the odor from whatever made the area wet. Before returning any products to the cabinet, wipe each item down. Consider storing your cleaning items together in a plastic bucket or bin. That way, everything is together and ready to go when you need to clean. It also prevents the wood cabinets from getting damp and damaged from leaks and spills.

Empty the contents and wipe the interior down with the vinegar-water cleaning solution. Make sure to clean the tops and bottoms of all shelving as well as the top, bottom, sides, and inside doors of the cabinet. Pay close attention to crevices where insect webs and egg nests can exist.

Sinks, Faucets, and Bathroom Countertops

By the time you finish cleaning the ceiling, walls, mirror, window, and cabinets, enough time has passed to return to the areas you prep cleaned earlier. Start with the sink and countertop. Begin by removing anything that sits atop the bathroom countertop and around the sink area. This includes toothbrushes, toothpaste, razors, soap, brushes, and any other personal grooming items that may be out. Any items left out in the open in the bathroom are subject to germs. They should be kept away from the toilet and should be cleaned weekly. Place them out of the way for now.

Bathroom sinks and countertops should be cleaned daily.

- Use water to rinse toothpaste, soap, and shavings down the drain after each use.

- Spray the countertop and sink daily with the vinegar-water cleaning solution to keep it clean and germ-free.

- After removing items away from the sink area, remove the towel initially placed around the faucets and knobs.

- Use vinegar-soaked towel to wipe faucets and surrounding areas. This eliminates lime and other hard-water deposits.

- If any residue remains around the base of the faucet or sink handles, use a cleaning toothbrush and vinegar to get in the hard-to-reach crevices.

- Spray vinegar-water cleaning solution on the counter, splashguards, and in the sink.

- Pour 3 cups of boiling water over the open drain that you had previously topped with baking soda and vinegar.

- Take a clean, soft cloth and wipe the countertop and the rest of the sink.

- If any hard-to-remove sticky spots or stains exist, use baking soda paste to remove them.

- For difficult stains, cover the area with the baking soda paste and let it sit for 15 minutes. After that, take a soft cloth and rub it over the stain using a slow circular motion until it goes away.

If you prefer the smell of lemon, sprinkle the stain with a tablespoon of regular table salt, and rub half of a lemon over the stain. *If you have surfaces that require special handling, refer to Chapter 14 for additional information.*

Cleaning Personal Grooming Tools

As mentioned previously, personal grooming tools left out on countertops or other areas in the in the bathroom are subject to germs. They should be kept as far away as possible from the toilet. Each week, clean these objects while you complete your other bathroom cleaning chores.

Toothbrushes

Toothbrushes, in particular, need to be kept away from the toilets for obvious reasons. For the best possible germ protection, keep toilet lids down when flushing and not in use, and place toothbrushes as far away as possible. The American Dental Association recommends the following steps to keep your toothbrush clean and free of bacteria:

- Never share toothbrushes.

- Rinse the toothbrush after each use; be sure to remove any remaining debris left after brushing. Soaking the toothbrush briefly in mouthwash may decrease germs, but do not let it sit there over time. Bacteria can grow in a cup.

- Do not store them in airtight containers. This could promote bacterial growth.

- Leave them out to air dry, but keep them from touching other toothbrushes, to prevent the spreading of germs.

- Routinely replace them every three months, if not sooner. Replace them sooner if bristles become worn or frayed. Additionally, toothbrushes should be replaced immediately after you recover from being sick.

- Using the microwave or dishwasher to clean your toothbrushes may get rid of some germs, but it may also damage the brush.

If you house toothbrushes in a cup or other toothbrush holder, clean these frequently as well. Since toothbrushes are frequently wet when they are put away, this area is a prime area for potential bacteria and mildew growth. Weekly, rinse these areas with hot water and wipe down with vinegar-water cleaning solution. For stubborn staining in a cup, sprinkle with 1 Tbsp. of baking soda and following with 2 Tbsp. of vinegar. Let it sit for one hour, then place cup in the dishwasher to complete the cleaning and disinfection process.

Hair-care tools and appliances

Brushes and combs

- Fill clean sink with warm water and 4 Tbsp. of baking soda, and mix thoroughly.

- Remove extraneous hair from combs and hairbrushes.

- Immerse hairbrushes and combs.

- Soak the hairbrushes and combs for 30 minutes.

- Rinse thoroughly with clear, warm water until no residue remains.

- Set them on a clean cloth until they dry.

- Wipe down the sink with another soft cloth to remove any remaining residue on the sink.

Hair dryers

Hair dryers accumulate hair and dust particles in their grills and filters. To remove dirt:

- Use a small cleaning scrub brush or cleaning toothbrush, then get larger particles out of the grill and filter areas.

- Use a small hand-held vacuum cleaner to remove the remaining hair and dust.

- If the appliance is particularly dirty, you can remove the cover with a screwdriver to clean the inside.

- Pick out any hair and lint, and wipe with a slightly damp cloth before reattaching the cover. Small appliances, such as hair dryers, work best when they are clean and lint-free.

Curling irons and flat irons

Hair irons get very dirty after repeated use, particularly when they are used in combination with hair styling products. The easiest way to clean these items is to do so while they are still warm.

- Unplug the appliance and let it cool slightly so you do not burn yourself.

- When it is cool enough to handle, run damp cloth over the surface to remove residue.

- If stubborn stains exist, spray a small amount of vinegar-water cleaning solution on the cloth and wipe it again until it is clean.

Rinse razors regularly

Clean razors are the most effective. They are also less likely to inflict cuts. Razors accumulate hairs when they are used. Additionally, if left out on the counter, they can gather dust and dirt particles as well.

- To eliminate shavings, rinse the blade under hot water with every use. There may still be some hair and lint in the blade.

- Take the blade off and soak it in 1 cup of hot tap water and 1 Tbsp. of vinegar for 15 minutes.

- Rinse the blade and dab it dry before replacing it to eliminate the possibility of rusting. Do this at least once a week. If the blade is in really bad shape, replace it.

Tackling the Toilets

Toilet bowl cleaners are particularly toxic. If they are ingested, the substance can cause vomiting, pulmonary edema, coma, or even death. This is a big concern around animals and small children. The toilet bowl is understandably where people tend to use their strongest chemicals. Unfortunately, by trying to eliminate germs, you end up creating other health issues instead. Most toilet bowl cleaners use some form of bleach. As I mentioned previously, bleach is dangerous on its own, but it is even more potent when combined with acid substances like ammonia. Urine contains natural occurring ammonia, so adding bleach to a toilet can result in toxic fumes.

Vinegar is the answer to the problem. It is an excellent cleaning agent and germicide.

- For general cleaning on a regular basis, spray the vinegar-water cleaning solution under the rim of the bowl, and let it sit for an hour before flushing.

- The vinegar solution will clean the toilet and surrounding areas.

- Wipe under the seat, around the rim, and all around the outside of the bowl. These areas carry the majority of the germs from waste products.

- If you are going to be out of town for a while, dump 2 cups of vinegar in your toilet bowls before leaving. Not only will this clean and deodorize, but it will prevent mineral stains from forming from standing water while you are away.

- Once a week, use the method described in the prep steps at the beginning of the chapter. After the baking soda and vinegar have stood in the toilet bowl for one to two hours, scrub the interior of the bowl with a toilet bowl brush along the water area.

- Flush to remove any lingering residue. This will eliminate germs and odors.

- If stubborn stains remain, use a baking soda paste on the stained area. While wearing gloves, smear the paste on any area that is stained and let it stand overnight, if possible.

- The next day, use a pumice stone to scrub off the baking soda and the remaining stains. Pumice stones are generally made from volcanic rock that is finely ground and molded for abrasive cleaning. They are commonly used for softening feet calluses and can be found in drugstores and discount chain stores in the health and beauty aisles.

Most toilet bowl cleaners contain toxic forms of acid. There are other acidic elements in homes that are non-toxic that can still get toilet bowl clean:

- Pour one can of cola in the toilet bowl. Let it stand for two hours. Cola products are acid-based. That acidity breaks down the dirt and grime stuck to the bowl. After two hours, scrub with the toilet brush and flush.

- Lemon juice is also acidic, and it has a pleasant smell. Fill a spray bottle with straight lemon juice, and squirt along the water line and under the rim. Let it juice stand for two hours before flushing. Use a toilet brush or pumice stone to scrub away any remaining residue. In addition to removing germs and stains, it serves as an air freshener.

- Instead of using toilet bowl drop-in products, place two denture-cleaning tablets in your toilet bowl at bedtime. If possible, leave them undisturbed overnight. They will fizz and clean the toilet bowl just as they clean teeth, and they are completely non-toxic.

In addition to cleaning the toilet interior, wipe the top, sides, seat, and floor surrounding the toilet with a vinegar soaked cloth. This will clean, disinfect, and deodorize the rest of the toilet.

Scouring the Shower

For best results, leave the plastic bag with vinegar attached to the shower-head overnight. This disinfects and removes any hard water mineral chemical build-up from the showerhead. If any form of lime deposits or corrosion exists on the handle leading up to the showerhead, use the faucet-cleaning method by soaking a towel in vinegar and drape it over the shower handle for at least an hour to loosen the grime.

If you do not have time to soak the showerhead in vinegar, you can scrub it with a homemade solution made from salt and vinegar. To make the solution, mix ½-cup of regular table salt and ½-cup of vinegar. Mix into an abrasive scrub. Apply with a sponge or scrub brush to loosen grime.

- If you prepped the shower walls by spraying them with vinegar, it will be easier to clean the surfaces now.

- Before you begin, be sure to remove all lingering products from the shower and tub area. It is easier to clean without having to work around soap and shampoo bottles.

- If you still have the shower curtain soaking in the washing machine, close the lid and finish the cycle.

- When you are done cleaning the shower, remove the curtain from the washer and gently shake out any excess wetness. It is ready to hang back in the shower — it does not require drying. If you use a white shower curtain that is a little dingy, you can hang it in the sun to brighten it.

- As the shower curtain cycle continues, tackle the shower walls, doors, and tub.

- To remove lingering dirt in the shower, use a soft cloth, sponge, or squeegee to wipe away residue left from the vinegar spray prep work.

- If it is too dry, spray more vinegar-water cleaning solution to the area in question. A squeegee is handy in daily cleaning.

- To decrease the amount of dirt and product build-up incurred, squeegee the shower walls after each shower. This will dramatically decrease the amount of work required to clean it weekly.

- If the grime and product build-up are substantial, consider using borax and a whole lemon. Borax is a natural laundry booster. You can find it in the grocery store with detergents and other laundry products.

- Cut the lemon in half and sprinkle borax powder on one half. Use the lemon half with borax as a scrubber on any stubborn dirt in the shower or bath.

- Rinse with hot tap water, and clear with a soft damp cloth.

- If your shower or tub area is tiled, the grout can become very dirty, but vinegar is safe to use.

- For stubborn areas, dip a cleaning toothbrush in vinegar or baking soda paste, and scrub as needed.

If your shower is in the tub, clean the tub area last. The vinegar-water solution will slide off the walls to begin working on the dirt in the tub.

- Clear the tub's drain area by pouring 4 cups of boiling-hot water down the drain.

- Next, take the vinegar-soaked towel off the tub faucet and handles, and wipe them down.

- Use a cleaning toothbrush to remove stubborn residue.

- Finally, run hot water from the faucet and clean the remainder of the tub with a soft, clean cloth.

- Spray additional vinegar-water cleaning solution as necessary.

- Finish by running a dry towel over the area to ensure no soap scum remains.

If you have shower doors instead of a curtain, clean the tracks with straight vinegar. This area is particularly prone to grime, mold, and mildew. Pour a small amount of vinegar onto the track and wipe with a clean cloth until the dirt is gone. If grime or stains remain, use baking soda paste and a cleaning toothbrush to loosen them, then wipe the dirt away. Clean the actual shower doors with vinegar water cleaning spray and a clean towel. If soap scum remains, sprinkle 1 Tbsp. of regular table salt onto half of a lemon and rub the lemon up and down the shower door until the soap scum is loosened. Rinse with a damp cloth or the vinegar-water cleaning solution.

The next morning, before using the shower, remove the showerhead bag and towel. Use the towel to wipe everything clean. The showerhead is now ready to use; no other action is required. To keep the bathing area clean, keep a spray bottle of vinegar water-cleaning solution in the bathroom. After each shower or bath, spray the solution over the walls, door, shower curtain, and tub. It will keep soap scum from building up, and it will prevent mildew from forming.

Bath toys and accessories

Disinfect children's toys, sponges, and accessories by soaking them in a clean tub with warm water and 2 cups of vinegar. Discard any items with mold.

204 The Complete Guide to Eco-Friendly House Cleaning

Down the drain

Bathroom drains frequently become clogged. Hair is the usual culprit in the bathroom sink and shower. Commercial products marketed to clean and clear drain clogs have acid in them and are very dangerous, particularly if they do not work. Plumbers will often charge extra to clear a drain if you have used one of these products before calling them.

Instead, use ½-cup of baking soda and 1 cup of vinegar on top of each drain weekly to help prevent bad clogs from forming. Let the mixture fizz and stand for one hour. Then clear by adding 2 cups of boiling water.

Additional Disinfecting and Deodorizing Not Necessary

People commonly reach for disinfectant sprays in the bathroom. They also use a variety of deodorizers and room fresheners in this room more than any other. Again, given the small nature of these rooms, this can create very toxic circumstances. If you use a vinegar-based cleaning solution regularly, it will accomplish all of your disinfectant needs.

In addition to spraying aerosol disinfectants, many people use a variety of deodorizers and other air-freshening products. These products often contain dangerous toxic substances, such as formaldehyde. Air fresheners work by deadening the sense of smell and masking one odor with a more pleasant one. Rather than using toxic chemicals, there are a number of other methods for making your bathrooms smell more pleasant.

First, consider making your own potpourri by placing a bowl of dried flower petals in a small jar. Add one to two drops of your favorite essential oil to the dried mixture. Add a lid with holes in the top to allow the smell to permeate the room without the mixture accumulating a lot of dust. If you do not want to use dried flowers, you can place a cotton ball in the jar soaked in your favorite essential oil. Lemon and lavender work particularly well in bathrooms. To make the jar look nicer, you can wrap a piece of fabric around the jar and secure it with a piece of ribbon.

Finally, the Floor

First, sweep the floors to pick up and discard any hair or other debris. Next, use a cloth soaked in vinegar to wipe down the baseboards around the room. This will clean any dirt residue on this area, plus it serves as a non-toxic pesticide. After the room is swept and the baseboards are clean, fill a bucket with hot tap water and 1 cup of vinegar. Mop the floor. Be sure to get the hard–to-reach areas behind the toilet, around the tub, under the sink, and under cabinets. If you have particularly tough-to-reach areas, consider getting on your hands and knees using a vinegar-soaked cloth. This is the best way to ensure you do not miss any areas. *To clean specific types of flooring, refer to Chapter 14.*

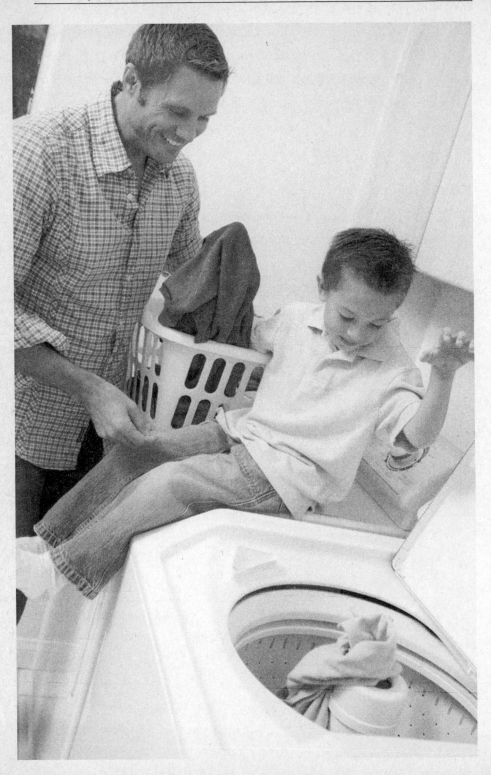

Chapter 10

Liberating the Laundry Room

"I want this dirt gone."

— Peter Lawler, American political scientist

What to Avoid and Why

Many commercial laundry products contain harmful chemicals on the EPA's list of dangerous chemicals to avoid. At this point in time, the labels on these products do not need to be as specific as other household products. Since the regulations are still relatively vague, higher concentration of toxic chemicals still exist in many of these substances. This is a concern because even in small quantities, these chemicals can cause everything from mild rashes to severe organ damage. Since these chemicals come in contact with our skin every day through clothing, bedding, and towels, it is important to be aware of particularly toxic substances. The chart below lists various laundry products you may use and some potential harmful health affects they can cause. As with all the products in your home, read all labels carefully. This chapter also provides many non-toxic alternatives for the traditional chemical-based items.

Laundry detergents

- **Naphthalene** — anemia, fatigue, nausea, vomiting, diarrhea, blood in urine, nasal and lung irritation, and skin discoloration

- **Phenol** — respiratory irritation, headaches, eye and skin irritation, liver damage, urine disturbances, and heartbeat irregularities

- **Phosphoric acid** — eye and skin irritation, lung damage, and central nervous system problems

- **Ethylenediaminetetraacetic acid** — hormonal disturbances, reproductive problems

Stain removers

- **Ammonia** — eye and skin irritation, lung damage, nasal irritation, sore throat, coughing, burns, and gastrointestinal upset

- **Benzene** — anemia, confusion, dizziness, drowsiness, rapid heart rate, immune system depression, vomiting, headaches, respiratory problems, and cancer

- **Bleach** — respiratory difficulties, headaches, skin burns, loss of consciousness, vomiting, lung damage, and asthma

- **Chlorine** — breathing difficulties, eye and skin irritation, nasal irritation, lung damage, and coughing

- **Formaldehyde** — joint pain, depression, headaches, chest pains, ear infections, chronic fatigue, and dizziness

- **Naphthalene** — anemia, fatigue, nausea, vomiting, diarrhea, blood in urine, nasal and lung irritation, and skin discoloration

- **Xylene** — eye and skin irritation, nasal and throat problems, breathing difficulties, lung damage, memory difficulties, stomach upset, liver damage, and kidney damage

Fabric softeners/dryer sheets

- **Alpha-terpineol** — headaches, skin irritation, coordination problems, and central nervous system disorders

- **Benzyl acetate** — coughing, nasal irritation, upper respiratory problems, and cancer

- **Benzyl alcohol** — headaches, dizziness, low blood pressure, nausea, vomiting, upper respiratory problems, and central nervous system disorders

- **Camphor** — eye, nose, and throat irritation, dizziness, confusion, nausea, and muscular problems

- **Chloroform** — headaches, dizziness, drowsiness, kidney and liver damage, skin irritation, vomiting, and upper respiratory problems

- **Ethyl acetate** — eye irritation, headaches, dizziness, confusion, anemia, liver and kidney damage

Spray starches

- **Formaldehyde** — joint pain, depression, headaches, chest pains, ear infections, chronic fatigue, and dizziness

- **Naphthalene** — anemia, fatigue, nausea, vomiting, diarrhea, blood in urine, nasal and lung irritation, and skin discoloration

- **Phenol** — respiratory irritation, headaches, eye and skin irritation, liver damage, urine disturbances, and heartbeat irregularities

Quick and Easy Laundry Tips

Laundry is a never-ending household chore. New dirty items require laundering each day. Here are a few quick tips that help keep the chore manageable:

- Keep laundry baskets in easy-to-reach locations in your home. Bathrooms and bedrooms are good options. Each family member should be responsible for getting dirty items to the laundry in a timely manner.

- If you have a separate room for laundry, consider designating separate sorting bins. Some possibilities are whites, lights, reds, darks, delicates, towels, and bedding.

- Treat stains immediately, and teach family members to do the same. Run stains under cold water or pre-treat them before throwing items in the laundry pile.

- Hang a clothing line inside and or outside and purchase a drying rack.

- Be sure to keep laundry areas free from dirt and dust.

- Place a bowl of baking soda in the laundry room to get rid of odors.

Preparing the Laundry Room

Whether you have an actual separate laundry room or a closet with a small washer and dryer in it, there are things you can do to prepare the space for maximum efficiency. To begin with, make sure the area remains clean. This area can become dust-ridden and full of lint very quickly. For the best results and cleanest clothes, keep the area clean as well. To do that in the simplest fashion, keep these tips in mind.

- Sweep the area regularly. Wet-mop it weekly.

- Once a month, pull out the machines and clean behind them.

- Periodically, wipe the walls down with vinegar water cleaning solution.

- Keep the lint trap free of lint by checking it after each load.

- Keep a trash can nearby for disposing of the lint. Empty it regularly.

- Do not keep unnecessary items cluttering the area. They will just collect dust.

- Wipe down machines and laundry products after each use.

- Do not let clothes stay in the room for an inordinate amount of time. Items may gather dust, become wrinkled, or possibly even become mildewed.

In addition to cleaning the area, prepare it for regular use. Keep things as simple and organized as possible, given any space restraints you may have. If you have the space, hang a clothesline in the room. Clothes will last longer if you hang them. Hanging a clothesline inside is helpful if you have outdoor space restrictions or weather issues to contend with where you live. Also consider putting up a drying rack. A tall drying rack is a nice addition to the laundry area. It is helpful for items that are not easy to hang, such as shorts.

If you have a lot of items that need to be ironed, such as shirts, blouses, pants, or skirts, consider leaving the ironing board up. It will make ironing easier if you do not have to take the iron and ironing board out every time you need to use it. Do not use the ironing board as a drying rack, however. Most ironing boards are metal and will rust if damp items are placed on top of them.

If your laundry area is in the basement, add a dehumidifier. It will help clothes dry faster. It will also keep the basement from getting musty and mildewed. If you have the space, consider designating separate sorting bins. You could have a separate hamper or bin for each load of laundry by type. Teach family members to bring their dirty items to the laundry space and sort it right into the appropriate bins.

If you have a large family, getting the laundry clean, dry, sorted, folded, and stored creates a daily challenge. To simplify it, add sorting bins for each person or room in the house. Fold clean items right into the appropriate bin. When the bin is full, take it to the room and put them away. This works particularly well for other family members. Designated laundry bins make it easier for family members to find their own items and put them away.

Cleaning the actual room

The laundry area can get dirty very easily. In order to keep the room clean, plan on deep-cleaning the space once a month. To do this, approach it the way you would any other room in the house. Start from the top-down.

This may be simple or difficult depending on your space. An upstairs laundry closet is going to be easier to clean than a full-size laundry room in an unfinished basement. Plan your time accordingly.

As in other areas of your home, when you clean the ceiling, you are primarily sweeping or dusting the area for cobwebs. Depending on the ceiling, use a broom first, then a damp cloth covered in vinegar-water solution. If your laundry is in an unfinished basement, be sure to clean around any pipes that may be overhead. Remember, vinegar is a natural insecticide, making it a great cleaning solution for this area. Get a big bucket of warm tap water and add 2 cups of vinegar, then do the following:

- Empty the area except for the machines.

- Wipe down the ceiling with a soft cloth covered in vinegar-water cleaning solution.

- Wipe down the walls with vinegar-water cleaning solution. Lint tends to create dust build-up on the walls in this space.

- If there are any windows, wipe them down with vinegar as well. Window wells in basements are common areas for insects to congregate. If you have curtains on the windows, take them down to throw them in the wash and wipe down the rod.

- Wipe down any baseboards with vinegar-water cleaning solution.

- Get a clean cloth and wipe down any shelves, cabinets, tables, and other fixtures.

- If you have a washing sink, clean it with vinegar and water as well.

- Run a damp cloth along the empty clothesline and over the drying rack rungs.

- Wipe down all cleaning product containers and organize them. Get rid of old, unnecessary items. Place the remainder in a bin, in a cleaned cabinet, or on a clean shelf.

- Sweep the floor first. Then, wet mop the floor with the vinegar-water cleaning solution. If you have rugs or mats on the floor, shake them out or throw them in the wash.

Bins for disposal

Consider a multiple bin system if you have the space. You can have one small bin for actual garbage — this includes lint. Add another small bin for recyclables. Laundry detergents and other plastic bottles can all be recycled. If you have a bin to collect them, there is a greater likelihood that they will not be accidentally thrown away. To keep these bins smelling fresh, sprinkle baking soda at the bottom each time you empty them. If you prefer adding a scent, you can place a cotton ball soaked in your favorite essential oil in the bottom of the bin instead.

You may also consider a few other bins as a way of organizing items that are not going to be put away with the other clean laundry. For example, consider adding the following items:

- A bin for sorting socks. Matching up socks can be a chore. You can place dry socks in a small crate to sort later when matches appear. Sort them once a week and put them in the appropriate person's laundry bin. As an alternative, consider placing socks with their matches in a small, zipped mesh bag before washing them.

- Assign a bin for items to be mended. Once a week, mend items before laundering.

- Designate a bin for items that are beyond mending that can be repurposed as rags.

- Also, consider adding a bin for items that will be donated.

Cleaning Your Appliances

In addition to cleaning the room itself, you need to also clean the machines you will use. All appliances require cleaning and maintenance. If machines are cleaned and properly maintained, they will last longer and work more efficiently. If you have older machines that cause problems with the laundry, clean them inside and out before you consider getting rid of them. If you take all the necessary cleaning and maintenance steps and they still do not work properly, look into purchasing new equipment.

When looking to purchase a new machine, research energy efficiency. Washing machines are a primary source of in-home water usage. Newer washers can handle a greater amount of items and use less water and power, making them more eco-friendly. For example, older washing machines use about 40 gallons of water per load. Newer machines with the Energy Star rating use only half that, or 20 gallons of water per load, making them much more environmentally friendly.

Washer

Washing machines accumulate dirt and product build-up over time. If you do not maintain your machine properly, it will not perform well, and you may end up with greasy spots on your clothing. If you have a new machine, read the maintenance instructions that came with the product and act accordingly.

If you have never cleaned your washing machine, now is the time to start. After you have cleaned the machine's exterior, move on and clean the interior.

- Run a complete cycle with hot water and a gallon of vinegar. Do not add any clothing or other items. This should be sufficient to clean even the dirtiest machines. When the cycle is complete, open the washer and wipe down the interior with a damp, clean cloth.

- If the machine walls suffer from specific stains, use baking soda paste to clean them off. For example, crayons left in children's clothes can stain washer and dryer walls. Baking soda paste takes the baked-on crayon off the washer and dryer. Use your cloth or a cleaning brush to get in and around the rims of the machine.

Dirt is not the only contributing factor that affects the cleanliness of your machine. Laundry detergents build up on the inside of the washing machine in the same manner shampoo creates soap scum in the shower. The vinegar cuts the greasiness of the product build-up and cleans the machine. If your home has soft water, you can eliminate this problem by using half the amount of detergent listed on the detergent bottle. Hard water requires a greater amount of product to create the same cleaning effect. Your water company determines your water type. If you have mineral deposit build-up on your faucets and showerhead, you most likely have hard water. If you are unsure, call your water company.

If you sometimes find that your washing machine emits an odor, it may need to be cleaned. Additionally, if you have a top-loading machine, leave the lid of your machine open when it is not in use. This will help it air out and decrease the possibility of odors.

Dryer

Clean dryers are not just important from an energy-efficiency point of view. A clean, well-maintained dryer can also prevent a house fire. According to the Consumer Product Safety Commission, approximately 15,000 house fires each year start from dryer lint. Lint is highly combustible and can accumulate behind the dryer for years. Add that to the dryer's heating element, and you have the potential for a fire that starts quickly.

A lint trap is a small mesh filter that catches extra fibers, called lint, from your laundry. The lint trap is located in different areas, depending on the dryer model you have. If the lint accumulates, it can obstruct airflow in the dryer, affecting the efficiency or your appliance and potentially creating a fire hazard.

Fire officials recommend cleaning out the lint trap each time you use the dryer. Once a month, you can also clean the trap with a little bit of soap and water. Make sure to get all of the soap off and wipe it dry before putting it back in the dryer. Additionally, make sure the dryer is in a well-ventilated area. Make sure air can flow around the back and both sides of the dryer. Keep the top clutter-free. Do not store items on top of it for maximum safety and efficiency.

Ironing boards and irons

When you clean the laundry area, make sure to check your iron and ironing board as well. They also accumulate dirt, dust, and grime. Most ironing board covers can be removed and thrown into the washing machine for cleaning. If not, spot-clean it with a towel or brush. If you do this, make sure to put a towel between the cover and board itself. Ironing boards are generally made from metal and can easily rust. In addition to the board cover, clean the underside of the ironing board and legs with a damp cloth to remove dust.

To keep the ironing board clean, never place wet clothes on top of it. Since most ironing boards are metal, this may cause the board to rust. If rust does form on either the iron or the ironing board, use baking soda paste to remove it. If the rust is extensive on the ironing board, use steel wool to loosen it. Make sure to get rid of rust before putting the cover back on the ironing board. The rust can bleed through to clothing when you iron clothing.

Maintain your irons properly for maximum efficiency. If the instruction manual directs you to use distilled water and you opt to use tap water, you may end up with mineral deposits. If there are many mineral deposits, you can clean the iron from the inside-out the same way you clean the coffee maker.

- Remove excess fluid from the water chamber and fill it with distilled vinegar.

- Turn the iron on and set it to "steam."

- Using the steam function, run the iron over an old towel or rag until all of the vinegar has evaporated. This should eliminate the problem.

- If any white spots remain on the iron, turn the iron off, and as it cools, rub a vinegar soaked cloth over the spots to remove them.

- If stubborn stains remain, use a baking soda paste on the iron when it is completely cooled.

If you have a problem with black marks on your clothing, scorch marks on the iron may be the problem. In this case, wait until iron is cool, and rub the face of the iron with a mixture made from equal parts of vinegar and salt. Gently rub until the black marks are completely removed from the iron.

Another source of dirt on an iron stems from ironing something that becomes sticky from the irons heat, such as a T-shirt decal. If this occurs, remove the sticky substance while the iron is hot. Run the iron over an old towel or rag until the substance is gone. If necessary, unplug the iron and rub the rag along the face of the iron as it cools.

Handling the hamper

The word "hamper" is derived from the British term meaning "wicker basket." In the United States, we use the word to identify the bin we use for dirty clothes. As a means of organization, have a centralized location for the dirty clothes hamper. The bathroom where people shower is a good place since people are usually taking off dirty clothing before they get in the shower. If you have multiple people in your home, you probably have a lot of laundry. To simplify the system, you may want to consider adding a hamper in each bedroom. With the exception of small children, each person can be responsible for getting their dirty items to the laundry area.

When you empty the hamper, check for lingering dirt and debris. Take a damp towel and run it over the inside and outside of the hamper before returning it to its designation. If odor is an issue, squirt a bit of lemon juice on the cleaning cloth and go over it again. If this does not solve the problem, consider sprinkling the bottom with a teaspoon of baking soda. If the hamper has a removable cloth insert, throw it in the washing machine to clean it. If it appears to have mold or mildew spots, soak the liner in equal parts vinegar and water before attempting to wash it. If the stains are not diminished, replace the liner.

If the hamper is plastic, wipe it dry before using it again. If it is made of wicker or cloth, place it in the sun to dry. Dampness can create mildew. Along those lines, be careful not to place wet towels or other items in the hamper among dry clothing. Mildew can ruin clothing and bedding.

Products and Alternatives

Government regulations and growing public awareness continue to create a need for alternatives to products containing harsh chemicals. Although companies are beginning to remake formulas that are less toxic, the majority of commercial products still contain many chemicals. There are other more eco-friendly solutions available if you know where to look.

Get it clean

One of the biggest problems with traditional commercial laundry products are the vague regulations concerning ingredients. The industry does not have the same standards that regulate the food and cosmetic industry. Therefore, product labels are less specific and much more difficult to interpret. A December 2008 report by Fox News℠ found that many companies use generic terms on their labels as a substitute for specific ingredients and amounts.

You may not be able to decipher the ingredients in the laundry products, but there are steps you can take to make doing the laundry a more eco-friendly task. When you consider eco-friendly laundry solutions, remember these hints:

- Cold water gets clothes clean. Plus, cold water uses less energy and costs less.

- Wait until you have a full load to run the washer. If that is not possible, use the lower setting so you only use an amount of water that is absolutely necessary.

Laundry detergents

Laundry detergents contain many chemicals, such as bleach and other whiteners. Some contain petroleum-based ingredients, and most commercial detergents contain some form of added fragrance. The added chemicals may be the source of unnecessary health risks, such as mild allergic reactions. Some may cause headaches, severe respiratory problems, or worse. Laundry detergents are commonly used because they are well-known and commercially marketed. There are, however, multiple alternatives to commercial laundry detergents. Here are a few:

- **Laundry soaps**: Laundry soaps are less toxic because they are derived from natural fats and minerals. The most common types of laundry soap are Ivory®, Zote®, and Fels Naptha®. They are available in the grocery store in the laundry product aisle. Many people use these soaps in conjunction with washing soda and borax to make homemade non-toxic laundry detergent.

- **Laundry washing balls**: Washing balls are very eco-friendly. They do not use harsh chemicals, last for numerous washes, and come in a recyclable container.

- **Soap nuts**: Soap nuts are the fruit of the Sapindus Mukorossi tree. It is a completely biodegradable, organic alternative to laundry detergent. Soap nuts are gaining in popularity in the United States and can be purchased at health food stores and on multiple Web sites. Three soap nuts in a mesh wash bag can wash up to ten loads of laundry.

Homemade Laundry Soap Recipe

Grate one bar of laundry soap into a container with a lid that can be tightly sealed after use.

Stir in ½-cup of all-purpose washing soda.
Mix in ½-cup of borax.
Use 2 Tbsp. in each full load of laundry.

Before using laundry soap, wash all items in washing soda alone. This eliminates chemical residue that may remain from traditional detergents.

Some laundry detergents can dull the look of fabrics over time. Making sure your washing machine is clean helps. Additionally, always use the correct amount of product as designated on the package. Here are some additional eco-friendly options for brightening your clothes:

- Add ½-cup of vinegar to the rinse cycle. It whitens as well as softens.
- Add ½-cup of salt with the wash.
- Add ½-cup of borax during the washing cycle.
- Add ½-cup of washing soda to the laundry.

Fabric softeners

Many products geared toward softening fabrics are highly toxic. Commercial products use multiple chemicals as softening agents and fragrances. These same chemicals may be very harmful, causing symptoms such as headaches, skin irritation, dizziness, nausea, allergies, asthma, confusion, and even cancer.

The chemicals that make synthetic fabrics softer actually have very strong, unpleasant odors. In view of that, manufacturers mask the chemicals with about 50 times as much fragrance as other products.

Rather than take a chance on exposing yourself and your family to unnecessary health risks, consider using a non-toxic means for softening your clothing and other laundry, particularly if you or other family members have sensitive skin or allergies. Try one of these non-toxic alternatives:

- Wash synthetic fabrics and cotton fabrics separately.
- Add 1 cup of vinegar to your wash cycle; this also helps with dryer static.
- Add ½-cup baking soda to your wash cycle.
- Use a non-toxic detergent with a built-in, soy-based fabric softener.

Getting it dry

There are more simple eco-friendly options for getting laundry dry than there are for getting it clean. No special products are necessary; all you need is air and time.

Just hanging out

Hanging your clothes to dry is one of the most cost-effective, eco-friendly changes you can make to your household-cleaning regimen. Household dryers are a huge environmental burden. They use a lot of energy and emit carbon dioxide. Consider the following alternatives to throwing everything in the dryer.

- Hang laundry on a clothesline outside. Fresh air beats chemicals.

- Hang items on a clothesline inside. The fresh air scent is missing, but in some areas, an outdoor clothesline is simply not an option.

- Use a drying rack. It is great for items that do not hang well.

- If you do not have space for a clothesline or drying rack, use the bathtub. Push the shower curtain aside and hang items on hangers along the curtain rod, if your rod is not a metal material.

Using the dryer

If you do not want to totally eliminate dryer usage, consider hanging most of your items. Saving the dryer for smaller items that are difficult to hang, such as socks and underwear. Consider hanging everything until it is mostly dry. Place items in the dryer for only 5 minutes to soften them and get out the wrinkles.

The controversy concerning dryer sheets

On an environmental level, dryer sheets are not biodegradable. They do not decompose and are rapidly filling our landfills, so they are definitely not eco-friendly. More importantly, dryer sheets are dangerously toxic. They contain chemicals that can lead to cancer, Alzheimer's disease, brain damage, liver disorders, and a variety of other nervous system problems. The traditional commercial paper dryer sheets coat laundry items with a film of artificial perfumes made from chemicals. Since the regulations are vague for the laundry industry, companies can get away with using very toxic chemicals in these products.

Problems arise because the coating stays on clothing and bedding, and eventually penetrates the skin. Chemicals that touch the skin get into the bloodstream and can cause serious health threats. Along those lines, fabric sheets are particularly dangerous because they contain multiple chemicals. Also, many individuals use multiple fabric sheets simultaneously for increased softness and fragrance, but the potential threat also increases dramatically.

Dryer sheet alternatives include:

- A ball of tin foil
- Dryer balls
- Tennis balls
- Reusable non-toxic cloth sheets

- Recyclable non-toxic dryer sheets
- A soft cloth with a couple of drops of essential oil

When ironing is necessary

To limit the amount of ironing you need to do, set a timer for your wash and take it out as soon as the cycle is complete. That will minimize wrinkles. Take care to hang items neatly. For example, be sure to fold pants along crease lines. This will help decrease the amount of wrinkles, thereby limiting the time it takes to iron the items.

To starch or not to starch

Homemade spray starch recipe: 3 Tbsp. of cornstarch mixed into 4 cups of cold water in spray bottle. Shake well before using. It works best on damp clothes. The concoction can be stored in the refrigerator for up to a week. After that, make a new batch.

All about dry cleaning

Today's business-casual dress policy requires far less dry cleaning than before. Regardless, there are times when dry cleaning is a necessity. Business suits simply do not look as professional if they are laundered at home. There are some items, however, that can be machine-washed despite the "dry clean only" label. Consider the item when making a decision about laundering.

Traditional dry cleaning fluids contain extremely toxic chemicals, including perchloroethylene (PERC), which is a known carcinogen. The chemicals can also cause liver damage, kidney damage, and nervous system disorders. The U.S. Environmental Protection Agency states that even the fumes from dry-cleaned items hanging in the closet are a major indoor air pollutant. Dry cleaning chemicals are very potent and the effects can linger for months. Currently, there are a few more environmentally friendly options.

- Water process dry cleaning
- Carbon dioxide cleaning
- GreenEarth® Cleaning

Before taking clothes to the dry cleaners, research all the facilities in your area. Call and determine which ones use eco-friendly cleaning methods.

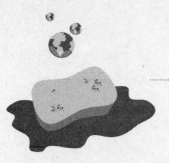

Chapter 11

Wrestling With the Rest of the House

"Laughter and tears are both responses to frustration and exhaustion. I myself prefer to laugh, since there is less cleaning up to do afterward."

— Kurt Vonnegut, American novelist

What to Avoid and Why

The chart below depicts general types of cleaning products used in various areas around the house. Different brands of products have different formulas. This a general list of harmful side effects that may possibly be produced from some of these types of products. Review all labels on your products before using them, and pay attention to any health-related side effects you may incur while using these or any other cleaning products.

Carpet cleaners

- **Ammonia** — eye, mucus membrane, and skin irritation; coughing; burns; asthma; and lung damage

- **Butyl cellusolve** — eye, mouth, and nose irritation; headaches; and vomiting

- **Naphthalene** — anemia, fatigue, nausea, vomiting, diarrhea, blood in urine, nasal irritation, lung damage, and skin discoloration

- **Perchloroethylene** — cancer, central nervous system disorders, dizziness, sleepiness, nausea, tremors and disorientation

- **Phosphoric acid** — coughing, nose and throat irritation, stomach cramps, vomiting, burns, liver damage, and kidney damage

- **Propylene glycol methyl ether** — eye, nose, and throat irritation; headaches; and nausea

Floor cleaners

- **Cresol** — liver damage, kidney damage

- **Formaldehyde** — joint pain, depression, headaches, chest pains, ear infections, chronic fatigue, and dizziness

- **Nitrobenzene** — headaches, nausea, vomiting, irritability, dizziness, drowsiness, liver damage, and muscle weakness

- **Perchloroethylene** — cancer, central nervous system disorders, dizziness, sleepiness, nausea, tremors, and disorientation

- **Phenol** — respiratory irritation, headaches, eye and skin irritation, liver damage, urine disturbances, and heartbeat irregularities

- **Toluene** — drowsiness, confusion, weakness, memory loss, nausea, loss of appetite, and hearing and color vision loss

- **Xylene** — eye and skin irritation, nasal and throat problems, breathing difficulties, lung damage, memory difficulties, stomach upset, liver damage, and kidney damage

Dusting sprays/furniture polishes

- **Ammonia** — eye, mucus membrane, and skin irritation; coughing, burns, asthma, and lung damage

- **Formaldehyde** — joint pain, depression, headaches, chest pains, ear infections, chronic fatigue, and dizziness

- **Naphthalene** — anemia, fatigue, nausea, vomiting, diarrhea, blood in urine, nasal irritation, lung damage, and skin discoloration

- **Nitrobenzene** — headaches, nausea, vomiting, irritability, dizziness, drowsiness, liver damage, and muscle weakness

Electronics cleaning products

- **1,1,1,2-Tetrafluoroethane** — headaches, skin irritation, dizziness, nausea, confusion, heartbeat irregularities, upper respiratory problems, and central nervous system depression

- **Ammonia** — eye, mucus membrane, and skin irritation; coughing; burns; asthma; and lung damage

- **Ethylene glycol** — liver and kidney damage, upper respiratory problems, skin irritation, and central nervous system issues

Fabric protection substances

- **Hexabromobiphenyl** — thyroid problems

- **Octabromodiphenyl ether** — thyroid problems and central nervous system disorders

- **Pentabromodiphenyl ether** — thyroid problems and central nervous system disorders

- **Perfluorinated compounds (PFCs)** — brain development problems, thyroid problems, neurological disorders, hormonal disturbances, and behavioral changes

- **Poly-chlorinated biphenyls (PCBs)** — skin conditions, neurological problems, and immune deficiencies

The Ceiling

Regardless of the room you begin in, you should always begin by straightening and organizing. It is much easier to clean a room that is picked up; you do not want to be stepping over scattered items to get to the area that needs to be cleaned. That being said, when you are ready to clean, start at the top and check the ceiling. Use a broom first, and sweep along the ceiling edges and in the corners to remove any cobwebs. Additionally, once a month, you should clean the entire ceiling. Climb on a ladder and wipe down the ceiling with a damp cloth covered in vinegar-water solution. If it is easier for you, you can use a damp mop to perform this step.

Windows, Walls, and Doors

Windows

- Clean windows simply with straight vinegar, using either crumbled newspaper or a soft cloth.

- First clean in and around all of the window sides and tracks; then use a clean cloth or newspaper for the actual window surface. Clean in a straight, up-and-down motion for streak-free windows.

Curtains and blinds

Curtains often are neglected, and they collect a lot of dust. Traditional blinds can be difficult to clean.

- If you have simple curtains, take them down and throw them in the washing machine once a month, and hang them to dry.

- If you have professional drapery, it is not that simple. For these, use a small handheld vacuum to remove dust. For extra-heavy dirt or grime, consider using a hand-held steam cleaner.

- For traditional blinds, the easiest method is to cover your hands with old socks that are dampened with the vinegar-water solution.

- Rub your sock-covered hands over each blind, one at a time, to collect the dust.

- When you are done, the socks can be washed in the washing machine.

Doors, baseboards, outlets, and switch covers

Doors and doorknobs accumulate a lot of dirt and germs, as they are touched constantly.

- On a regular basis, use the vinegar-water cleaning solution and a soft cloth to get these areas clean and disinfected.

- Do the same for light switches in every room.

Once a month, using the same vinegar and water solution and a soft cloth, clean all of the baseboards and outlet covers.

- Make sure nothing is plugged in at the time, and be careful not to get fluid in the outlets.

- Wait at least one hour before plugging items back into the outlet to allow the area to dry.

At this time, also evaluate any pictures and other wall hangings. These items collect dust and spider webs. The best way to clean them is with a damp cloth. Any chemicals or even too much water can damage the finish.

Walls

Do not forget your walls. When you approach seasonal cleaning, take a rag soaked in vinegar and water, and wash down the walls in each room. Another option is doing this in one room each month. Remember that in addition to being a great cleaning agent and disinfectant, vinegar acts as a natural pest-deterrent.

The Living Room and Family Room

These areas serve as the center of the home. For best results, keep areas picked up and organized daily. Remember to clean forgotten areas that may harbor the most germs, such as lamp switches and remote controls.

Upholstery

Stain guards may seem like a good idea when you are furniture shopping, but they are actually bad for the environment and can cause harmful side effects. Conditions include eye and skin irritation, dizziness, nausea, and fatigue.

For the best results in getting stains out, deal with it as soon as it occurs. That may sound obvious, but if you have children, you realize that you may not always be notified as soon as it happens. Most substances will come out with dish soap and water and a little bit of elbow grease. *For more detailed information on cleaning specific stains, refer to Chapter 15.* If your seating has throw pillows, spot-clean them as necessary. Additionally, shake them outdoors to remove excess dust. If family members have allergies or asthma, throw pillows into the dryer with a damp cloth to remove dust particles.

Fireplace and gas heaters

Real fireplaces require regular cleaning and maintenance to prevent them from becoming household fire hazards. After you have used your fireplace, wait until the next day to clean it out. Do not touch hot ashes.

- After they have cooled, use a small metal shovel and scoop out the ashes into a metal bucket.

- If you have used real wood, consider saving the ash and adding it to your garden soil. Since it is derived from plant material, it consists of essential nutrients that are good for plant growth.

- After removing the ash, you can clean any areas of the brick or stone that have blackened from soot.

- To remove this, add 1 cup of vinegar to a bucket of soapy water.

- Dip a hard-bristled brush in the water and scrub until the soot is gone. If any stains persist, try rubbing half of a lemon coated in coarse salt over the area to remove the stain.

- If you have family members with allergies or asthma, you may want to consider burning eco-friendly logs that contain no chemical additives. They are made from recycled materials and tend to be cleaner than real wood.

Real fireplaces also require regular chimney maintenance. For best results, contact a chimney service at the end of the season. If you have not done this, at least contact them before using again for the next season. Before cleaning a gas fireplace, make sure the gas valve is turned off. Follow the manufacturer's instructions before attempting to turn the gas on again. Make sure the fireplace is completely cool before attempting to clean it. Pay particularly close attention to the burner and control compartment, which should always be kept clean. To do this:

- Vacuum it out at least once a year.

- Logs for gas fireplaces are very fragile, but they also must be cleaned.

- In order to get dust and debris off the logs, gently wipe with a very soft cloth or a soft bristled brush. If any logs are broken, do not use the fireplace, as this poses a safety issue.

- Any problems with logs that are cracked or positioned incorrectly may create carbon build-up, which can damage the unit.

- The exterior can be cleaned with a soft wet cloth. Warm tap water is sufficient for surface cleaning. Any other chemicals may harm the finish.

Home Electronics

Dust is a big problem when it comes to electronics, because it gets into areas you cannot see and may potentially damage the working parts by causing them to overheat. The most important thing is to read the manufacturer's instructions. Different equipment requires different cleaning methods and precautions.

Note: If you do not already have a special place for all of your manufacturer's instruction manuals, designate one now. It will save you from having related problems in the future. It can be a file in a file cabinet, a box, or a drawer. Regardless of where you keep it, place all the instructions in one place. That way, you will always know where to look.

For best results in cleaning electronics, use a soft cloth or microfiber duster. They are the safest. Paper towels are not a good idea, as they can scratch delicate screens. Remember, paper is made from wood. Aside from being eco-friendly, using rags and cloths makes monetary sense because they can be washed and used again.

The first thing you should always do before cleaning any product that uses electricity is to unplug the mechanism before cleaning it. It is much safer. For the most part, a dry microfiber duster or a slightly damp cloth will get the job done safely and efficiently. If you do use an all-purpose cleaning product or the vinegar-water solution, always put it on the cloth. Never spray anything directly on or into one of your electronics, as it may damage the components. If you have hard-to-reach dusty areas, gently swab the area with a dry cotton swab to lift the dirt out.

The piano

To get the most out of your piano, you should have a professional clean and tune it once a year. Additionally, if you are able to keep the keys covered, do so to avoid unnecessary extra dust in the interior of the piano. Other than that, clean your piano weekly as you would the rest of your furniture. A damp cloth is sufficient for the exterior surfaces. To disinfect the keys, use a soft cloth dampened with the vinegar-and-water cleaning solution.

Wood furnishings

Run a damp cloth over wood furnishes regularly to remove dirt and dust. To polish wood, use a combination of 1 cup of olive oil and ⅓-cup lemon juice, shaken in a spray bottle. Spray a small amount of the polish on a soft cloth and rub into wood.

The Dining Room

Most designated dining areas contain a table, chairs, and some form of buffet or hutch. Clean the tables off after every meal with a damp, soft cloth.

- If the table is wood and you want to polish it once a week, use a couple of drops of extra virgin olive oil and rub them gently into the wood of the table until it is polished but not sticky. Do not use too much, or it will remain wet.

- If you encounter a water-ring stain on your table, the best remedy is plain white (non-gel) toothpaste. Rub it on the ring and let it set for an hour. At that point, take a soft dry cloth and gently rub it over the stain in small circular movements until the stain is gone.

- If you encounter a larger white stain from hot take-out food, such as pizza, immediately hold a steam iron over the white stain. It will lift the stain off the wood.

Silver

Real sterling silver cannot go in the dishwasher; it will ruin it by taking the finish off. There are many chemical-filled silver polishes on the market, but they are all toxic, messy, and smelly. Some of them may even harm your silver if you are not careful.

- Instead, if your silver is only covered in a small amount of tarnish, you can clean it with baking soda paste. Make a paste out of three-parts baking soda to one-part water.

- Using a soft cloth, rub the mixture onto the tarnished area of the silver in a gentle circular motion.

- Rinse with clear warm tap water as the paste starts to blacken.

If the silver is very tarnished and has not been polished for more than a year, it may require more work. In this case, prepare a small plastic tub or large roasting pan to soak the silver pieces in.

- Line the bottom of your tub or pan with aluminum foil and place tarnished silver on the aluminum. The aluminum reacts with the silver and helps remove the tarnish, so make sure that all of the silver is touching the aluminum. It will not work on pieces that are just sitting on top of other silver pieces.

- Next, boil 8 cups of cold tap water, ½-cup baking soda, and 3 Tbsp. table salt in a pot on the stove. You may need to adjust this amount, depending on the amount of silver pieces you are cleaning. Make sure you have enough to cover all of the silver.

- Once the baking soda and salt are dissolved, and the water comes to a full boil, turn off the stove and carefully pour the mixture over the silver pieces. The combination of baking soda, salt, and the aluminum makes the tarnish disappear almost instantly.

Crystal and glassware

If you have crystal or glass vases, or other glass pieces with stains on them, you can clean them with warm vinegar and uncooked rice. Place 1 Tbsp. of dry, uncooked rice in the bottom of the item and fill the remainder with warm vinegar. Let the item sit with the vinegar and rice in it overnight. In the morning, shake the rice into crevices to scrape any remaining dirt off the glass, and pour the mixture out into the sink. Rinse with warm tap water and dry with a clean, soft cloth.

China

If your china is plagued with stains, such as coffee or tea, use a vinegar and salt solution to clean them off. Pour ¼-cup of salt into 2 cups of vinegar and mix thoroughly. Soak the affected china in this solution for 24 hours. Use a damp cloth to rub the stain away. Clean with dish detergent and rinse with warm tap water. This also works with stained glassware.

Home Office

Computers, printers, fax machines, and telephones

Dust is big problem for any machinery, and computers and other office equipment are no exception. Remember to check the manufacturer's instructions before attempting to clean any equipment.

- Turn everything off before cleaning anything.

- Use a soft cloth or microfiber duster.

- Use a cotton swab for small, hard-to-reach areas.

- Use a small amount of vinegar-water cleaning solution to disinfect items that are touched frequently, such as keyboards and telephones.

- Do not push on the computer screen. Touching them too hard can damage LCD monitors, plasma screens, and laptop screens.

- Dust in and around all equipment.

Cleaning the keyboard

The keyboard on a traditional computer or a laptop collects a lot of dirt and dust. But products on the market to clean them are full of chemicals. The most popular product is a can of compressed air. The air blows the particles out from under the keys, but most of the brands of compressed air now have an additional chemical added, a bitter additive to prevent anyone from using the product in an inappropriate manner. Instead, anyone who uses the air to clean the keyboard ends up with fingers that taste and smell bad for a very long time. There are numerous blogs online of people searching to find out what ailment they have incurred, only to discover that a strong, long-lasting chemical added to the compressed air causes the affliction. The simplest alternative solution is to dip a cotton swab into vinegar. Make sure it is only damp and not dripping. Run the dampened cotton swab along the edges of each key slowly and carefully to get as much dust and dirt out as possible. Additionally, keep the keyboard covered when not in use.

The Bedroom

Mattresses

Regardless of the base material, all mattresses benefit from regular cleaning and maintenance. Mattresses actually collect more dust than any other area of your home. But because it becomes imbedded in the mattress and is not visible, most people neglect it. To keep your mattress in good shape, perform the following:

- Add a mattress cover.
- Wash linens weekly.
- While the linens are off, vacuum the mattress.
- Every three months, flip the mattress.
- To clean stains, sprinkle with baking soda and rub with a soft cloth soaked with vinegar. Scrub with a cleaning brush to remove soil. Allow mattress to dry completely before returning linens. This works particularly well for disinfecting and deodorizing urine stains.

Pillows

Over time, pillows accumulate skin, dust, fungus, mold, and mildew. It is disgusting when you think about it, and is a huge problem for allergy and asthma sufferers. Manufacturers recommend replacing pillows every three to four years. Economically and ecologically, though, that may not always make sense. Here are some suggestions for getting the most mileage out of the pillows you do have. There are numerous types of bed pillows and pillow coverings available on the market, depending on personal choice. Consider the following when it comes to having clean pillows.

Synthetic pillows

- For allergy- and asthma-sufferers, synthetic foam pillows are the best option. They are hypoallergenic, easier to clean than natural materials, and are generally less expensive.

- Consider purchasing zipper pillow protectors. These pillowcases completely encase pillows and will keep pillows cleaner. They can be removed weekly and washed with the rest of the bedding. If you do not have pillow protectors, you can still keep your pillows cleaner by using two pillowcases. Put them on the pillow in opposite direction so the pillow is completely covered.

- Once a month, or sooner if someone has been sick, throw the entire pillow in the washing machine. Always read the manufacturer's care instructions. Different types of pillows require different care. For example, some synthetic pillows are machine washable and can be placed in the dryer. Memory foam pillows, however, need to air-dry on a flat surface for the best results.

- Do not put more than two pillows in the wash at one time. Set the machine to the delicate cycle. When you start the water, add the detergent to mix it well before adding the pillows. Add 1 cup of vinegar to the rinse cycle to soften, eliminate static cling, and to disinfect and deodorize the pillows.

- When air-drying any pillow, place on a flat surface on top of a towel. The towel will absorb the moisture as it dries. Be sure to flip the pillow periodically.

Feather / natural-filling pillows

- Once a week, air out your down pillows by hanging them on a clothesline. Shake them out to fluff them before putting them on your bed. If the weather does not cooperate, toss them in the dryer for 20 minutes with dryer balls or clean tennis balls.

- Most pillows are machine-washable. According to Heloise's Hints in *Good Housekeeping*, even feather pillows can go in the washing machine, as long as they do not have any holes in them. To dry feather pillows, throw them in the dryer with two dryer balls or clean tennis balls to fluff the pillows. Make sure the pillows are thoroughly dry before using them. Wet feathers will smell and may create a mold or mildew situation. Feathers can sometimes develop an odor if left out in the sun to dry as well.

- If you decide to handwash your pillows, be sure to use a mild detergent. It does not take as much detergent if you are washing them by hand. Rinse thoroughly to remove any remaining the soap residue.

Children's Spaces

The nursery

It is particularly important not to use toxic chemicals in the nursery. Babies are the most susceptible to harmful chemicals around the home because their brains, lungs, and immune systems are not yet fully developed. They also breathe faster, causing more chemicals to enter their lungs.

- Open the windows while cleaning.

- Using the top-down cleaning method, clean the walls and ceiling with vinegar-water solution.

- Wipe down furnishings with vinegar and water as well.

- Vinegar is safe for cleaning teething rings and other toys, too. It is non-toxic, but it is strong enough to disinfect these items.

- Wash stuffed toys in clear, unscented, non-toxic laundry detergent.

- Wash bedding weekly or more often if necessary, using clear, unscented laundry detergent.

- Vacuum carpeting, upholstery, and curtains weekly to minimize the accumulation of dust.

Toy/recreation room

- Small children are susceptible to spreading germs because of their habits. Vinegar and baking soda will disinfect and deodorize their special spaces, as well as all of their toys.

- Many plastic toys can be cleaned in the dishwasher. Place smaller toys in a mesh bag and sit on the top rack of the dishwasher.

- If stickers or decals are no longer wanted on a painted surface, saturate the corners and edges with white vinegar. Scrape it off with a spatula or plastic card.

- After a child recovers from illness, soak all washable items in a basin containing 2 quarts of warm tap water mixed with ½-cup of baking soda.

- Unless cleaning instructions prohibit machine-washing, place small plush toys in the washing machine and wash in warm water. Tumble dry.

- If stuffed toys require surface cleaning only, brush with a vinegar-water cleaning solution.

- If dust mites or lice are an issue, place stuffed toys in dryer on high heat for 20 minutes. Then, place in a large garbage bag tied tightly — this deprives organisms of oxygen, thereby killing them. Leave toys in the bag for one week to ensure organisms are all gone. Remove from bag and place in dryer for 20 more minutes with a clean, wet towel before returning them to children.

Playgrounds and pools

Mix 1 cup of baking soda in a bucket containing 1 gallon of warm tap water. Use solution to clean baby pools, playground equipment, and children's lawn furniture. If items do not appear to be clean, follow by wiping with the vinegar-water cleaning solution.

Basement

- Basements sometimes have musty odors. Clean walls with vinegar-water cleaning solution.

- Musty carpet smells may indicate mildew growth. If the carpet harbors moisture, mold or mildew can grow. Sprinkle carpet with baking soda, and use a dehumidifier.

- Window wells in basements tend to collect dust, webs, and bugs. Be sure to clean each month with hot water and vinegar.

- Clean furnishings as you would in the rest of the house.

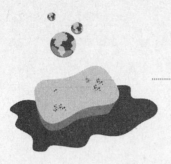

Chapter 12

Eco-Friendly Pet Care

"These aren't just pets. These are a part of the family. You miss them when you're away. You worry about them. They really are important parts of your life."

— Linda Lingle, Governor of Hawaii

General Information

Like children, pets are particularly susceptible to toxic cleaning supplies. Instead of chemical-based products, use non-toxic remedies for pet-related cleaning issues. In 2008, the Environmental Working Group (EWG) conducted a case study on dogs and cats. They collected blood and urine samples from 20 dogs and 37 cats. The animals displayed traces of 48 out of the 70 industrial chemicals tested. The study showed that more than half of these chemicals had a concentration of 2.4 to 5 percent higher in pets than in humans. These chemicals are commonly found in food packaging, heavy metals, fire retardants, and stain-proofing and stain-resistant coatings. This study suggested that the nature and behavior of domesticated animals puts them at an elevated risk for toxic chemical exposure.

Removing pet odors

There are a number of things that can contribute to animal smells around the house, including everything from outside dirt to excrement. Here are some suggestions for eliminating pet odors around the house:

- Change litter box on a regular basis.
- Add baking soda to the litter box.
- Add coffee grounds to the litter box.
- Sprinkle baking soda on pet fur and brush it out.
- Clean animal accidents with vinegar to neutralize odor.

Removing skunk odor

If your pet encounters a skunk and is sprayed, use the following non-toxic solutions for getting rid of the odor:

- Bathe the animal in tomato juice.
- Bathe the animal in vinegar, and use vinegar to clean any household area that has been affected.
- Place charcoal around affected areas to absorb excess odors.

CASE STUDY: GETTING RID OF LINGERING PET ODORS

Michelle Sharp
Property Owner and Landlady
Mechanicsburg, PA

Michelle Sharp and her husband, Dr. Allen Levy, own and manage multiple properties. When a tenant leaves, they do most of the cleaning and preparation for the next tenant by themselves.

I own a rental property in a small town in central Pennsylvania. The home was built in 1900 and has gorgeous, old features. It has been converted into two rental properties. One of my favorite features is the charming, wide-paneled hardwood floors that I discovered after we bought the property. In preparing it for tenants, we wanted to rip out the old, worn carpeting.

CASE STUDY: GETTING RID OF LINGERING PET ODORS

My first tenant owned cats. These longhaired cats lived in his bedroom, as did their two large cat litter boxes. Needless to say, when he moved out at the end of a one-year lease, the beautiful antique floors reeked of cat urine and used litter. To my dismay, I found out why the odors were so strong: Some of the litter box contents poured over the sides during use and had lodged between the wide, uneven cracks of the floors. This further imbedded the smell into the floorboards.

At first, I tried the traditional hardwood floor cleaners. The hardwood floors are the original floors, so I did not want to take a chance on ruining them. I started with Armstrong® Wood Floor Cleaner. My floors looked nice, but the smell remained. I followed with another product and did not get any better results. Eventually, I became frustrated and switched to a bleach-and-water mixture, which also did not work. When the smell had not dissipated after hours of scrubbing, I started looking for alternative solutions — air fresheners and candles — and they just masked the smell and made it worse.

Finally, I consulted a hardwood floor installer before I attempted to clean the wood again. He recommended using a mixture of vinegar and water, and I was willing to try anything. The odor still lingered, but it had significantly improved. Since the vinegar seemed to help remove the odor, I went one step further: I placed large bowls of vinegar around the house to absorb any remaining smell.

Using the vinegar and keeping the windows open finally worked. If I had known to use the vinegar in the beginning, I could have saved myself a lot of time and frustration.

Deterring pets

To keep pets, in particular cats, off windowsills or specific furnishings, spray the area with vinegar. Additionally, the scent from vinegar also deters cats from scratching the upholstery. Be sure to test the spray of vinegar on an area of fabric that will not be seen, in order to keep it from staining any fabric.

Flea control

Fleas can be a household nightmare. If they get into the home, they will get in all the soft fabrics and bedding. Not only will they bite pets, but they will bite humans as well.

In trying to protect their household pets from pests, Americans spend billions of dollars on flea and tick products. Some products are safer than others, but many of these products create harmful chemical residues that linger on pet fur and in the home. According to the National Resources Defense Council (NRDC), these pesticides remain on animal fur for several weeks. Additionally, the levels of pesticide are almost 1,000 times higher than the levels deemed acceptable by the EPA. This amount of toxic chemicals may cause cancer, brain damage, and serious nervous system disorders.

A paper released by the NRDC in April 2009 stated that two chemicals commonly found in flea collars are particularly dangerous: tetrachlorvinphos and propoxur. These are two of the most lethal pesticides still legally available. The danger extends beyond the pets to owners as well. In particular, children who play with pets can get these chemicals on their hands, and if they touch their mouth or eyes prior to washing them, they may accidentally introduce poison into their systems.

The NRDC study suggested the following hints on protecting your pets and your family from these chemicals:

1. Bathe pets weekly with pesticide-free pet shampoos, rather than using chemical-ridden flea collars.

2. Use flea combs between baths.

3. Launder pet's bedding in hot water.

4. Vacuum carpets daily to eliminate potentially hidden flea eggs.

5. If you still want a chemical flea control product, discuss alternatives with your vet. For example, consider using the kind that is

dispensed in pill form. They are less toxic and do not leave chemical residue on animal fur.

6. Check the labels of the flea and tick control products before you purchase them. Avoid products that list tetrachlorvinphos or propoxur as the active ingredients. Also avoid permethrin-based products, and those containing the chemical amitraz.

7. For a more comprehensive list of brand-name pet products, their ingredients, and the corresponding health risks, refer to **www. greenpaws.org**.

Make Your Own Non-Toxic Kitty Litter

Consider making your own kitty litter. Homemade kitty litter helps you save money and avoid unnecessary chemicals.

1. Shred one entire newspaper into strips and wash it in soapy water, using sink detergent.

2. Stir newspaper strips and soapy water until it is the consistency of oatmeal.

3. Take newspaper concoction and place it in a colander.

4. Rinse with clear, warm tap water.

5. Add enough baking soda to newspaper to soak up any moisture.

6. Wearing rubber gloves, knead the substance like bread dough, squeezing out excess moisture. The substance will start to dry and break up.

7. Break the substance into small, pebble-sized pieces. Crumble until it is all in small bits.

8. Lay it out on a screen to dry. It may take several days until it is completely dry.

9. When it is dry, put about 2 inches of the paper crumbles in the litter box, scoop out solids daily, and change it once a week.

Chapter 13

Dealing With Dirt Outdoors

"Weed — a plant whose virtues have not yet been discovered."

— Ralph Waldo Emerson, American essayist, philosopher, and poet

What to Avoid and Why

The information below depicts the general types of products used around your home's exterior. Different brands of products have different formulas. This list contains chemicals typically found in these types of products and the potential side effects that may occur from using them. Always review the labels on any product before using it. Additionally, pay close attention to any health-related side effects you may incur while using these or any other products.

Lawn fertilizer and maintenance products

- **Arsenic** — skin irritation, nausea, vomiting, cancer, birth defects, heart rate irregularities, liver damage, kidney damage, and impaired nerve function

- **Cadmium** — nose and throat irritation, coughing, headaches, chest pains, muscle cramps, vertigo, weakness, and kidney disease

- **Lead** — central nervous system disorders, muscle weakness, increased blood pressure, anemia, brain damage, kidney damage, reproductive issues

- **Mercury** — skin irritation, mood swings, memory loss, mental disturbances, central nervous system issues, muscle weakness, and kidney damage

- **Phosphates** — drowsiness, nausea, stomach cramps, osteoporosis, kidney and liver damage

Weed control products

- **Glyphosate** — headaches, nausea, vomiting, dizziness, muscle weakness, drowsiness, lethargy, agitation, anxiety, difficulty breathing, blurred vision, confusion, and memory loss

- **Phenoxy herbicides** — cancer, liver damage, and skin disease

- **Triazine** — reproductive problems, birth defects, and developmental delays

- **2, 4-D** — anorexia, lethargy, nausea, vomiting, diarrhea, loss of muscular coordination, and cancer

Pesticides

- **Benzene** — anemia, confusion, dizziness, drowsiness, rapid heart rate, immune system depression, vomiting, headaches, respiratory problems, and cancer

- **Creosote** — eye irritation, confusion, skin irritation, upper respiratory problems, kidney and liver damage

- **Esfenvalerate** — reproductive problems, developmental issues, nervous system disorders, and cancer

- **Formaldehyde** — joint pain, depression, headaches, chest pains, ear infections, chronic fatigue, and dizziness

Deck cleaners and stains

- **Bleach** — respiratory difficulties, headaches, skin burns, loss of consciousness, vomiting, lung damage, and asthma

- **Formaldehyde** — joint pain, depression, headaches, chest pains, ear infections, chronic fatigue, and dizziness

- **Phosphoric acid** — eye and skin irritation, lung damage, and central nervous system problems

- **Sodium hydroxide** — upper respiratory problems, nose and throat irritation, pulse irregularities, lung damage, vomiting, eye irritation, and chronic skin irritation

Cleaning Out the Garage

- Clean the garage on a regular basis. Ideally, the garage should be cleaned once a month., If that is impractical, plan to tackle it quarterly. Keep in mind that the longer you go between cleanings, the more difficult the task will be.

- Take everything out. Wipe each item with a wet rag. Continue to clean items, walls, and floor with soap and water. If residue remains anywhere, use a cloth soaked in the vinegar water cleaning solution.

- Be sure any chemical-based products are packed tightly and out of reach from children and pets.

- If you are disposing of chemical-based products, be aware of your municipality's regulations. Never pour chemicals down the drain or throw them in with your regular trash. *See Chapter 16 for some of the general rules and call your municipality for specifics.*

- Place a box of baking soda on the shelf to absorb odors.

- Do not put away wet items, such as camping gear, umbrellas, and car carriers. Towel-dry wet items and sprinkle with baking soda before packing them away.

- For oil spills on concrete, mix equal parts baking soda and corn-starch and sprinkle liberally over stain. Let mixture sit overnight, then vacuum clean. For tougher spots, use baking soda paste and scrub with a cleaning brush.

Cleaning Your Vehicle

- To clean your vehicle, use mild dish detergent and water. Be careful not to use any other toxic cleaning products that will end up on the lawn or back in your water system.

- Wash the windows of your car with vinegar for streak-free shine. Keep a spray bottle of vinegar and water in your car with a clean, dry cloth for long trips.

- Freshen the inside of your car by placing a few drops of essential oils on a cotton ball and putting in the car trash bag or ashtray.

- If your vehicle is cursed with bad odors from any bodily fluids, remove the odor by placing an open container of coffee grounds on the dashboard overnight. Used coffee grounds are great at absorbing odors.

Eco-Friendly Lawn and Garden Care

Cleaning the lawn mower

- First, empty the gas tank and disconnect the spark plug wire so the lawn mower does not start while you are cleaning it.

- Rinse the mower's top with warm water.

- If dirt remains, use mild dish detergent, water, and a clean cloth to clean it off.

- Remove any grass and dirt clumps off the bottom. If they are not removed, it can negatively affect the mower's performance.

- Make sure mower is completely dry before refilling the gas tank and returning the spark plug.

- Also check the oil, fuel, and air filters, as well as the blade, before using the mower.

Lawn care

- Keep mower blades between 2½ and 3 inches high for the best results. You will have to mow more often, but keeping the grass longer helps the grass resist drought and disease.

- Instead of bagging the grass and making unnecessary waste, use the scraps to naturally fertilize the lawn. If you have a mulching mower, the clippings go into the roots to help the health of the lawn.

- If there are more than a few weeds, add 2 cups of coarse salt to 1 gallon of boiling water. It takes a little time and patience, but the weeds will be gone for good. Salt is actually very potent, so do not pour it on any plants that you want to live.

- Vinegar is another non-toxic weed killer. For the best results, spray weeds with straight vinegar when you know it will not rain for a couple of days.

Tending the garden

- Pour table salt directly on slugs, ants, snails, and other small pests that may plague your garden.

- Instead of using commercial fertilizer on your flowers, add vinegar to your watering can to brighten your flowers and improve the acidity of your soil.

- Vinegar will deter unwanted insects as well.

- If you have pots that are stained, soak them in warm water and vinegar. The stains will be gone, and the vinegar smell will deter insects.

- Use a rain collector. Place an empty bin in the yard to collect rainwater. Be sure to cover with a lid when not in use, because standing water attracts mosquitoes and the potential for West Nile disease. Use the rainwater as needed to water plants.

Create a compost pile

A compost pile comprises your household's organic and kitchen refuse. Let it sit and decompose, and it can be used in fertilizing and conditioning a garden or yard. According to the EPA, composting accomplishes the following:

- Suppresses plant diseases and pests

- Reduces or eliminates the need for chemical fertilizers

- Promotes higher yields of agricultural crops

- Facilitates reforestation, wetlands restoration, and habitat revitalization efforts by amending contaminated, compacted, and marginal soils

- Cost-effectively remediates soil contaminated by hazardous waste

- Removes solids, oil, grease, and heavy metals from storm water runoff

- Captures and destroys 99.6 percent of industrial VOCs in contaminated air

- Provides a cost savings of at least 50 percent over conventional soil, water, and air pollution remediation technologies

Residential compost piles use food and yard waste that decomposes and is later used as nutrient-rich fertilizer. In order to create your own compost pile, you first need to designate space. It can be outdoors or inside, depending on available space and personal preference. Compost piles require three basic ingredients:

- **Browns**: Provide carbon for the compost and come from outdoor waste materials such as dead leaves, branches, and twigs

- **Greens**: Provide nitrogen to the pile and consist of items such as grass clippings, vegetable waste, fruit scraps, and coffee grounds

- **Water**: Provides moisture and helps break down the other organic matter

The following lists what can and cannot be used in residential compost.

Allowable compost materials:

- Cardboard rolls
- Clean paper
- Coffee grounds and filters
- Cotton rags
- Dryer and vacuum cleaner lint
- Eggshells
- Fireplace ashes
- Fruits and vegetables
- Grass clippings
- Hair and fur
- Yard trimmings
- Wool rags
- Wood chips
- Tea bags
- Shredded newspaper
- Sawdust
- Nut shells
- Leaves
- Houseplants
- Hay and straw

Unacceptable compost materials:

- **Black walnut tree leaves or twigs** — May release substances that might be harmful to plants

- **Coal or charcoal ash** — Might contain substances harmful to plants

- **Dairy products (such as butter, egg yolks, milk, sour cream, yogurt)** — Create odor problems and attract pests such as rodents and flies

- **Diseased or insect-ridden plants** — Might survive and be transferred back to other plants

- **Fats, grease, lard, or oils** — Will create odor problems and attract pests such as rodents and flies

- **Meat or fish bones and scraps** — Will create odor problems and attract pests, such as rodents and flies

- **Pet wastes (such as dog or cat feces, soiled cat litter)** — May contain parasites, bacteria, germs, pathogens, and viruses harmful to humans

- **Yard trimmings treated with chemical pesticides** — Might kill beneficial composting organisms

If these guidelines are followed, the compost pile will not invite pests or smell bad. There are multiple methods for creating an outdoor compost pile, such as this one posted on the EPA Web site:

1. Select a dry, shady spot near a water source for your compost pile or bin.

2. Before you add your brown and green materials, make sure larger pieces are chopped or shredded.

3. Cover your composting area with a 6-inch layer of brown materials.

4. Add a 3-inch layer of green materials and a little soil or finished compost.

5. Lightly mix the two layers above.

6. Top with a 3-inch layer of brown materials, adding water until moist.

7. Turn your compost pile every week or two with a pitchfork to distribute air and moisture. Move the dry materials from the edges into the middle of the pile. Continue this practice until the pile does not re-heat much after turning.

8. Your compost will be ready in one to four months, but let the pile sit for two weeks before using.

CASE STUDY: COLLEGE COMPOSTING

Ken Shultes, Vice President of Facilities
Dickinson College
Carlisle, PA 17013
shultes@dickinson.edu

Ken Shultes is the vice president of facilities at Dickinson College in Carlisle, Pennsylvania. Dickinson has been working toward eco-friendly maintenance principles for the last seven years. The college has received numerous honors for their practices, including the LEED Gold award; an A-rating (the highest rating provided) from the Sustainable Endowment Institute; being named one of the Sierra Club's "Cool Schools" for ecoenlightenment; earning a place on Princeton Review's Green Honor Roll; and receiving the Governor's Excellence Award in 2009 for their composting program.

We adhere to the principles of green cleaning, and we use environmentally friendly cleaning products. Additionally, our grounds crew is specially trained in the use of pesticides on campus. We use them as sparingly as possible. Our maintenance department is well-versed in the college's commitment to sustainability and efficiency in all areas of maintenance, and they are fully on-board with it; they understand that they play an important role in our success.

Waste reduction is an important aspect of our sustainability program in the area of campus operations, and we have extensive recycling and composting programs on campus. We recycle cardboard, co-mingled materials, paper, and construction debris. We also compost our yard waste. More important, we compost 100 percent of the food waste coming out of the dining hall. This practice earned us the Governor's Excellence Award in 2009. Since 2002, we have used daily deliveries of salad bar scraps from the cafeteria, about 50 pounds a day.

CASE STUDY: COLLEGE COMPOSTING

In 2005, we placed rainbow-colored trash cans in the college dining hall to kick off the campus-wide composting initiative. At that time, students had the opportunity to scrape their own plates into these bins during breakfast seven days a week. Garden workers then collect these bins each day. During that fall semester, we expanded the program to include lunch. When students came back from winter break in 2006, we had added new compost bins featuring a tile counter to rest trays on while scraping plates. The compost bins are collected each day by garden workers and brought to the campus's new composting facility site located near campus.

The student garden is partnering with Facilities Management to manage the compost piles. While the student gardeners collect, transport, and incorporate new food waste, facilities workers supply our piles with woodchips made from tree, shrub, and leaf debris from campus. Facilities Management is also responsible for turning the piles for effective and timely decomposition. This campus-wide effort has significantly reduced the amount of food waste that Dickinson College sends to our local landfill. The addition of recycled napkins has also helped us with this initiative. It is estimated that the student garden composts approximately 800 pounds of food waste each week.

Currently, Facilities Management makes these decisions. They are always responding to the requests and ideas of our extended campus community. Our Facilities Management department has always had efficiency, safety, health, and financial sustainability as a primary objective. Over the past five to seven years, this commitment has accelerated, and the primary rationale for moving in the direction of environmental sustainability has evolved to include environmental soundness as the primary driver for our decisions.

Outdoor Living Spaces

Eco-friendly picnic practices

When it is time to have a picnic outdoors, do not reach for a chemical insect repellent. There are numerous substances in your cupboard that will accomplish the same thing.

- Set out a bowl of vanilla extract, or dab some on your pulse points. Vanilla is a natural mosquito repellent.

- Instead of using the noisy bug zapper, put a few drops of either lavender or peppermint essential oil on a cool, outdoor light bulb nearby. When the light is turned on, the oil will naturally repel the insects.

- Additionally, soak cotton balls with peppermint or lavender oil, and place them in sealed jars with holes in the lids. Place the jars on food tables and eating areas.

Decks

- Composite decking combines waste wood fibers with recycled items, such as plastics, and lasts for years without requiring chemical staining and specialized maintenance products.

- Use vinegar to clean stains off all deck materials. For particularly difficult stains, scrub with baking soda paste and a cleaning brush.

- Avoid pressure washers for wood decking; it can cause the wood to splinter.

Screened porches

- To clean the screened porch, first use a large-bristled paintbrush to remove larger debris.

- Follow by dipping the paintbrush in to a bucket of vinegar-water cleaning solution. Brush solution all over screens and wood encasement.

- Take a soft, clean, damp cloth, and rub over the screens and wood to remove remaining dirt. Wring out cloth and dip in plain warm water as needed.

- The vinegar will repel insects and handle early signs of mildew.

Brick patios and walkways

- Fill a bucket with warm water and vinegar. Use a cleaning brush to scrub brick areas in outdoor living spaces. Baking soda paste works on difficult stains. Use the garden hose to rinse. The vinegar and baking soda are non-toxic and will not harm your lawn or garden when washed from the brick pathways.

- Be sure to brush off any excess water. Standing water can leave a white residue on bricks.

Outdoor furniture

- Clean furniture with a bucket of vinegar-water cleaning solution, a cleaning brush, and a dry towel or rag. Vinegar does not harm the surface, and it will act as a natural insect repellent.

- Along those lines, put five or six drops of either lavender or peppermint oil in 1 gallon of warm water and use it to wash down the outdoor furniture before a party. It will help keep the insects away from the food and the crowd.

- For difficult stains, use baking soda paste and a scrub brush. Rinse well with warm water and set in the sun to dry.

The grill

- While the grill is still warm, scrap off large chunks of food.

- Use a baking soda paste to remove remaining burnt food from the grill rack. Use it on a cooled grill and let it set overnight. The remnants will wipe away easily with a damp cloth the next day.

- Sprinkle baking soda on grease spills near the grill for safety and easy, non-toxic cleaning.

- The grill's exterior may also be safely cleaned with baking soda paste.

Chapter 14
Surface Cleaning
Simplified

"Clean the air! Clean the sky! Wash the wind! Take stone from stone and wash them."

— T. S. Eliot, British poet

This chapter addresses the various surface areas throughout the house. Since numerous material types exist for flooring, carpeting, and countertops, this chapter includes specific eco-friendly cleaning approaches by surface type.

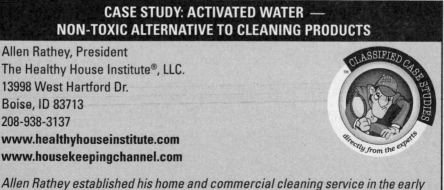

**CASE STUDY: ACTIVATED WATER —
NON-TOXIC ALTERNATIVE TO CLEANING PRODUCTS**

Allen Rathey, President
The Healthy House Institute®, LLC.
13998 West Hartford Dr.
Boise, ID 83713
208-938-3137
www.healthyhouseinstitute.com
www.housekeepingchannel.com

Allen Rathey established his home and commercial cleaning service in the early 1980s. After ten years of first-hand experience, he transitioned from cleaning to consulting, providing advice and marketing services through his communications

CASE STUDY: ACTIVATED WATER —
NON-TOXIC ALTERNATIVE TO CLEANING PRODUCTS

company. In 2004, he created **www.housekeepingchannel. com**, a Web site devoted to faster, healthier housekeeping. In 2005, he purchased the rights to The Healthy House Institute (HHI) from its founders, John and Lynn Bower. He is now the president of HHI, a source of up-to-date information to assist homeowners in making and keeping their homes healthier. HHI also includes a 31-member advisory board consisting of professionals from health and medical fields, health sciences, home building and remodeling, architecture and design.

Water is a universal solvent. It actually dissolves more substances than any other liquid. It is also a unique substance because it comfortably exists in all three forms of matter: liquid, solid, and gas, in a relatively narrow temperature range. Add to that, the fact that it is naturally occurring and pH-neutral, and you have the perfect base for a cleaning product. Of course, in most cases, it is just that: the base. Manufacturers may all start with the same base liquid, but they add chemicals to make it their own product. The problem is, research continues to strongly indicate that exposure to chemicals, even at low levels, may pose long-term risks to human health and the environment.

The truth is, the added chemicals are not always necessary. Water and microfiber cloths work in a wide variety of applications, and are readily available and safer. Additionally, new technology exists to improve the cleaning power of water without adding chemicals. It is a form of electrolysis, or "activation" of the water.

Activating the water involves adding a charge of electricity to your regular tap water. The charge enhances the water electrically and turns it into a better cleaning product. The science of electrolysis dates back to scientist Michael Farraday (1791-1867). The basic process requires two electrodes placed in water. The first electrode is connected to the positive end of a power source, while the other is connected to the negative end.

Adding electricity in a special chamber to water causes the water's molecules to break down into positively and negatively charged ions. These charged ions used in cleaning will bond to dirt, making it easier to lift from the surface. In some cases microscopic oxygen bubbles form, adding an additional element for dirt removal.

Studies have shown this technology to be effective as a mild, all-purpose cleaner for glass, stainless steel, granite, marble, and other washable surfaces. In some cases, it has been proved to effectively sanitize hard surfaces.

CASE STUDY: ACTIVATED WATER — NON-TOXIC ALTERNATIVE TO CLEANING PRODUCTS

The Healthy House Institute provides information on products and services available to those interested in making their home environments healthier. They do not personally endorse any products. If you are interested in learning more about water activation, please refer to the following sources:

For both consumers and commercial cleaning:

Activeion Cleaning Solutions
21308 John Milless Drive
Rogers, MN 55374 USA
866-950-4667
www.activeion.com

For commercial cleaning:

Tennant
www.tennantco.com/na-en/

Handling Various Wall Surfaces

Wood paneling

- Mix ½-cup of olive oil with ½-cup of white distilled vinegar, and 2 cups of warm tap water.

- Pour into a clean, empty spray bottle.

- Spray a small amount of the liquid onto a clean, dry cloth.

- Using cloth, rub over wood paneled surface in even, up-and-down strokes.

Repairing scratches on paneled walls

- For light scratches, rub olive oil over surface to fill in the area. The scratch will be virtually imperceptible.

- For deeper, more obvious gouges, mix two drops of iodine with 1 cup of cider vinegar and stir well.

- Use a small paintbrush and brush over scratched surface. Adjust the amount of iodine as needed. Use less for lighter wood and more for darker wood finishes.

Painted drywall

- Painted drywall is easy to clean. Use the vinegar-water cleaning solution and a clean cloth to wipe down walls. For stubborn stains, rub baking soda paste over the stain. Rinse with water, and follow with the vinegar-water cleaning solution.

- If you are repainting the surface and get excess paint drips on the windows, wipe away immediately and follow with vinegar-water cleaning solution to remove the remainder of the paint residue.

- If fresh paint smell is an issue, add 1 drop of extract per gallon to the paint can before using it. Be sure to stir it well. Use lemon extract for white or ivory paint, and vanilla extract for all other colors.

Dealing with wallpaper

- Use vinegar-water cleaning solution and a clean cloth to wipe down walls. For stubborn stains, rub baking soda paste over the stain. Rinse with water and follow with the vinegar-water cleaning solution.

- To strip wallpaper, add 1 cup of vinegar to a gallon of hot tap water. Dip clean dry cloth into vinegar-water solution and soak paper with liquid. The acidity of the vinegar helps break down the glue, making the paper come off quickly and easily. If paper is stubborn, add more vinegar.

All About Flooring

Worn and dingy carpeting

- Mix 1 cup of white distilled vinegar into 1 gallon of warm tap water.

- Dip edge of broom into liquid solution and brush gently over worn carpet surfaces.

- Allow to dry naturally.

Carpet odors

- Change vacuum bag.

- Add a cotton ball soaked in essential oils, such as clove, lemon, orange, or eucalyptus. The scent will permeate the carpet and freshen the house in a safe, non-toxic manner.

- If you prefer, you can add a spiced tea bag, some crushed dried flowers, or cinnamon to the new bag before vacuuming.

- For persistent smells, sprinkle carpet with baking soda and let it sit for 30 minutes to absorb odor. Then, vacuum as usual.

Carpet stains

- Treat stain immediately by blotting excess fluid with a clean, dry towel.

- Continue until no color appears on a clean spot on the towel.

- If stain persists, add club soda to the area and continue to blot with a clean, dry towel to lift stain.

- If stain remains stubborn, spray it with vinegar-water cleaning solution and let it sit for one hour. Blot dry to remove the remainder of the stain.

- To remove candle wax drippings from carpeting, lay newspaper down on top of the wax. Get the iron, turn it on, and set it on low. When it is warm, run the iron over the newspaper on top of the wax. The newspaper will absorb the melted wax, lifting it off the carpet. Use vinegar to remove the remainder of the stain. *Refer to Chapter 15 for specific types of stain treatments.*

Carpet shampoo

- Mix ¼-cup of castile liquid soap with 3 Tbsp. of warm tap water. Using a wire whisk, stir until mixture foams. Rub foam on stained areas of carpet. Let it sit for 30 minutes, and rinse with water. Blot away excess with a clean, dry cloth, and follow by shampooing carpet with vinegar and water solution.

- Instead of using chemical-laden carpet shampoo, make your own eco-friendly version. Add ½-cup of vinegar to 1 gallon of water and put it in the carpet-cleaning machine. Follow manufacturer's instructions for using the machine.

- If you have your carpet professionally cleaned, ask commercial carpet cleaning company to use only water, baking soda, steam, or club soda.

Flooring

General flooring tips

- To remove scuffmarks, wipe with a cloth dampened with vinegar.

- For stubborn marks and grease spills, make a paste of equal parts baking soda and water, and wipe with a damp cloth. If area is cloudy, follow with vinegar and wipe clean.

- For grease spills, sprinkle baking soda on the area, and wipe with a clean cloth and warm tap water.

- Do not use washing soda on waxed flooring, as it will ruin the wax finish.

Wood flooring

- For sealed wooden floors, mix together 2 cups of white vinegar and 2 cups of olive oil. Using a clean, dry cloth or a mop, rub into the wooden floors to get them to shine.

- If the floors are natural, unsealed hardwood, substitute straight linseed oil for the vinegar and olive oil solution. Allow it to soak in for an hour, and repeat for the best results.

No-wax flooring

- Mix 1 cup of vinegar into 1 gallon of warm tap water.

- Dip mop into liquid solution to clean no-wax flooring.

- For best results, use a clean cloth to get under cabinets, in crevices, and around edges.

Linoleum and vinyl flooring

- The vinegar and water flooring solution will clean linoleum as well.

- For stains on linoleum, apply area with a baking soda paste made of equal parts of baking soda and water.

- Let it sit for one hour, then scrub.

- Finish by mopping floor with vinegar-water solution.

Ceramic tile

- Mop with a solution of 1 gallon of warm water and ½-cup of vinegar.

Cleaning Those Countertops

General counter surface tips

- Never use acidic substances, such as vinegar or lemon juice, on marble or granite surfaces, as it will ruin the stone.

- Do not use washing soda on fiberglass or aluminum surfaces, as it will ruin the finish.

Corian counters

- Harsh chemicals can ruin Corian®. For general spills and light cleaning, use only water.

- For disinfecting and dealing with stains, sprinkle the countertop with baking soda and gently rub with a damp, soft, clean cloth.

- If stains persist, use a mixture of diluted hydrogen peroxide. The mixture should consist of equal parts of water and peroxide.

Marble counters

- Use plain water for general cleaning.

- Anything acidic can ruin marble surfaces. This includes orange-scented cleaning products and even vinegar.

- For best results, use diluted hydrogen peroxide.

- If you need an abrasive scrubbing agent to clean a specific caked-on mess, use baking soda paste. Be sure to rub gently.

Tiled surfaces

- The tile itself can be cleaned with vinegar-water cleaning solution.

- If a staining agent colors the grout, use club soda and a clean cloth.

- If club soda does not remove the grout stain, vinegar and baking soda paste is a viable alternative.

Stainless-steel surfaces

- Boiling-hot water works best at dislodging food and grime from stainless steel; plus, it will not scratch the surface.

- If additional cleaning is necessary, dissolve 4 tsp. of baking soda in 2 quarts of warm water. Stir well, and use soft cloth to clean and polish finish.

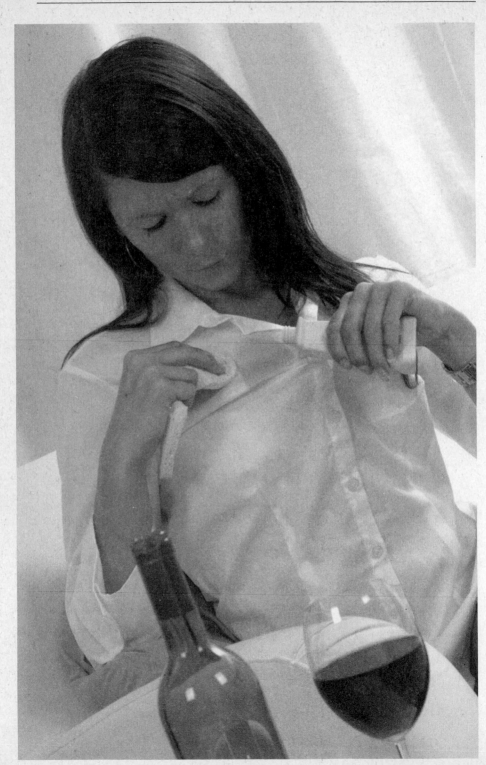

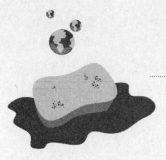

Chapter 15

Conquering Specific Stains

"Out, damn'd spot! Out, I say!"

— William Shakespeare, English playwright

Stains are inconvenient, but even the most cautious individual has to deal with them eventually. The most important ingredient is patience. Most stains are completely removable with proper timing, the right ingredients, and the patience to work with the stain until it disappears.

What to Avoid and Why

Many commercial stain removers contain non-biodegradable toxic chemicals and fragrances that may cause migraines, upper respiratory problems, and hormonal disturbances. There are some manufactured options that are more eco-friendly than others. You may want to consider these options if you have exhausted the alternatives and still cannot remove your stain.

Basic Tips

- In whatever means you have available at the time, treat the stain immediately. At the very least, use water or club soda to keep the stain from setting. As soon as you are able, pre-treat or soak the item, depending on the type of stain. The following information explains different types of stains and ideas for eco-friendly stain removal.

- Always blot the stain — never rub it. Rubbing can cause the stain to spread. If treated immediately, many stains can be removed simply by blotting with a white cloth. The cloth soaks up the stain, essentially transferring it into the cloth.

- Always review the laundering instructions on a garment before attempting to wash or treat a stain. Certain fabrics require specific care.

- In the interest of protecting your clothes, always start with the mildest possible treatment first. If that does not work, try something else.

- Never combine chemical stain-removing products. For example, the combination of items containing ammonia and those containing bleach could produce hazardous fumes.

An Eco-Friendly Stain Removal Kit

As with most of your cleaning product options, you probably already have virtually everything you need to remove even the most stubborn stains. Here is a list of items to store in a basket in your laundry room. There are some additional items you can use to fight stains that need to be refrigerated, such as milk and heavy cream. You may want to consider making a copy of these pages and placing them in the basket for easy access and review.

- Baking soda — deodorizes, whitens, and removes grease-based stains
- Borax — removes acidic and protein-based stains
- Castile soap — removes many grease-based stains
- Club soda — removes acidic-based stains
- Cornstarch — removes grease-based and protein-based stains
- Hydrogen peroxide — whitens
- Salt — removes grease-based stains
- Vinegar — deodorizes, disinfects, and whitens
- Washing soda — deodorizes and removes grease-based stains
- Large jug of tap water
- Set of white dishtowels whose sole purpose is stain removal
- Dull putty knife or other scraping mechanism for caked-on stains
- Eye dropper

Additionally, eggs, heavy cream, and lemon juice will help take out certain specific stains. Keep these items in the refrigerator until needed.

Protein-Based Stains

Protein-based stains include baby formula, blood, dairy products, cream, dirt, feces, urine, and vomit. Use detergent, not soap, on these stains, and always scrub and soak in cold water before washing. Be careful not to accidentally add heat to these stains, because any type of heat will set a protein stain. This includes washing it in hot water, running it through the dryer cycle, excessive scrubbing, or ironing over it.

Making Your Own Stain Remover

Different types of stains require different types of treatments. This explains why commercial stain removal products do not work on all stains. Once you know what kind of stain you have, it will help you determine what kind of approach you need to remove it. Here is a recipe for a homemade stain remover spray that will work on any protein-based stains.

- Mix ½-cup of borax powder with 8 cups of cold water.
- Put mixture into a spray bottle.
- Shake vigorously before each use.
- Spray mixture onto the protein-based stains as necessary.
- Let stain remover set on stain overnight for best results.

Oil-Based Stains

Oil-based stains are obviously marks originating from oily substances. These include, but are not limited to, automotive oils, butter, cooking oil, face and hand creams, food grease (such as bacon, mayonnaise, or pizza), hair products, and salad dressing. To remove oil-based stains, you need a de-greasing agent that will soak up the grease and hot water. Unlike protein stains, oil-based stains will not set with heat. Baking soda is an excellent non-toxic degreasing agent and, when used as a paste, will remove most oily stains.

Tannin Stains

Tannin is a natural substance found in numerous plants, such as grapes, oak, and tea leaves. Examples of tannin stains are red wine, mustard, coffee, and tea. Theses stains also require hot water to remove them. Do not use bar soap to remove tannin stains, as this actually will set a tannin stain.

Try This First

Luckily, there are numerous non-toxic household ingredients to aid in stain removal. But before using any of them, try to get the stain out with a little bit of cold water and a couple of clean, white dish towels. If it is a new stain, this will work most of the time. Put a couple of drops of cold water on the center of the stain and blot with the first white towel. Place the other towel underneath the stain on the other side of the fabric. Press in and soak up as much of the stain as possible. Continue by moving the towel around to clean spots to soak up more of the stain. Blot and press on both sides of the fabric containing the stain until most, if not all, of the stain has vanished. Complete the task by normal laundering.

Nature's Bleach

Commercial bleach is toxic and harsh on the environment. So what do you do if white items are yellowed or stained beyond repair? Hang them on a clothesline in the sun: It acts as a natural whitener and brightener. Women who hang their baby's white cloth diapers in the sun to air them out have discovered an added benefit — stain removal. After hanging directly in the sun, yellowed diapers look new again. Years ago, women hung their whites in the sun intentionally to keep them white and bright.

Stain Removal Guide by Stain Type

Alcohol

- Rinse stain in cold water immediately. Rub vinegar into stain and let it set for two hours before washing in cold water.

- If that does not work, mix 1 cup of borax in the washing machine with cold water. Soak garment in solution until stain lifts, then complete the rest of the washing cycle.

Baby formula

- Make a paste out of equal parts of baking soda and water, and place on the stain.

- For best results, allow the pre-treatment to set overnight.

- If the stain is not a new stain, soak for 30 minutes in warm water and washing soda before laundering.

- Launder as usual.

Beer

- Dab stain with vinegar as soon as possible.
- If it is a large stain, soak it in vinegar overnight, then wash in cold water.

Blood

- As soon as possible, rinse bloodstains with cold water. This should eliminate most, if not all, bloodstains.

- For difficult bloodstains that have not been attended to promptly, soak the item in cold water and 1 cup of dissolved table salt. After soaking for two to three hours, rinse with vinegar and wash normally.

- If the dried bloodstain is stubborn and does not come out with the prior methods, try using a borax paste mixture. Make a borax paste mixture with equal parts of borax and water, press it on the stain, and let it sit overnight. Brush the excess off with a cleaning brush in the morning and machine wash in cold water.

Candle wax

- Place garment in a sealed plastic bag and place it in the freezer for one hour.

- Once the wax is hardened, scrap it off with a metal spatula or putty knife. Be careful not to cut the garment.

- Place a clean, dry rag under the garment, run a warm iron over the garment, and repeat until the stain is gone. Wash normally.

Chewing gum

- Rub gum with ice; gum will flake off.
- Launder as usual.

Chocolate

- Scrape off any unabsorbed food. Treat stain with heavy cream and let it sit for one hour, then rinse with cold water and wash normally.

- If this does not work, treat the stain with vinegar and hang it on the clothesline until the stain disappears.

- Both of these methods work well if the stain is treated quickly. If this does not work, treat the stain with a couple of drops of watered-down hydrogen peroxide, and soak the item in cold water for several hours until stain lifts.

Coffee

- Run cold water over the coffee stain immediately.
- Treat with a couple of drops of vinegar, and let the garment sit for several hours.
- Launder normally in cold water.
- Alternatively, you can make a stain remover out of one egg yolk and ½-cup of warm tap water. Pour the egg mixture over the stain and let it sit for one hour. Launder normally.

- If the stain still requires additional treatment, use a paste made from equal parts Borax and water to treat the stain, and then launder.

Cosmetics

- Pre-treat makeup stains with a paste made from equal parts of borax and water.

- Let paste sit on clothing overnight, then launder as usual using cold water.

Crayon

- Crayons are made from wax; therefore, initially place the stained item in the freezer to harden any remaining wax.

- When the waxy substance hardens, scrape it off with a putty knife.

- Make a paste out of equal parts of baking soda and water, and put it on top of stain.

- Leave baking soda paste on stain overnight, then wash with hot water.

- If pieces of crayon go through the washer and/or dryer, it will cause a problem for all other laundry that follows it until it is cleaned off the sides. Baking soda paste will remove crayon on the insides of the machines. After removing the crayon stains off the machine, be sure to run a load of towels through the machines first to ensure that the crayon is completely gone.

Colas/dark-colored soft drinks

- Blot excess liquid from front and back of material to soak up stain.
- Run cold water over stain. If necessary, soak garment in cold water overnight.

- Launder in the hottest water appropriate for fabric type.
- If stain persists, repeat the process.

Cough syrup

- Run cold water over the stained area.
- Blot dry with a clean, dry, light-colored cloth to absorb the stain.
- Repeat process from the other side of the fabric.
- Continue until no more color is coming on to the clean cloth.
- Pour vinegar on both sides of the stain and let it sit overnight.
- Launder normally in cold water.

Dairy products (such as cheese sauces)

- Blot excess stain out with a towel.
- Run cold water over stain. If necessary, soak in cold water and mild detergent overnight.

Deodorant/antiperspirant

- Dilute stain by pouring vinegar over it.
- Let the garment sit overnight and launder as usual.

Egg

- Blot off egg liquid with clean dry towel.
- Soak in cold water and mild detergent for one hour and launder as usual.

Fruit juice

- Apply a paste made from equal parts of borax and water to neutralize the acidity of the stain. Cover entire stain with the paste.

- Let borax sit on stain for one hour, and follow by pouring hot water over it.

Grass

- Mix 1 cup of white vinegar with ½-cup of boiling-hot tap water, and pour onto grass stain.

- Let the stain sit overnight, and wash in cold water.

- If stains are stubborn, add a couple of drops of eucalyptus essential oil and work into stain. Let it sit overnight, and repeat the vinegar and water process.

- Launder per garment's instructions.

Grease

- Pour boiling-hot water on grease stain.

- Sprinkle dampened stain with baking soda and let it set overnight.

- Machine-wash with warm water.

- If oily stains persist, fill washing machine with warm water and 16 ounces of cola. Let the washing machine drum-mix it well, then add mild detergent and wash per garment instructions.

Ink stains

- Pour any variation of white milk (whole, 2 percent, or skim) over ink stain and blot excess fluid off.

- Let it set overnight and wash in cold water.

- If stain persists, add a couple of drops of rubbing alcohol on the stain and blot until stain bleeds and fades.

- Wash in cold water.

Ketchup

- Run cold water over the stained area.
- Blot dry with a clean, dry, light-colored cloth to absorb the stain.

- Repeat process from the other side of the fabric.
- Continue until no more color is coming on to the clean cloth.
- Pour vinegar on both sides of the stain and let it sit overnight.
- Launder normally in cold water.

Lipstick stains

- Run cold water over the stained area.
- Blot dry with a clean, dry, light-colored cloth to absorb the stain.
- Repeat process from the other side of the fabric.
- Continue until no more color is coming on to the clean cloth.
- If the stain is not getting lighter, add a drop of olive oil to the area to loosen the stain, and wait for one hour.
- Repeat the cold-water, towel-blotting process.
- Pour vinegar on both sides of the stain and let it sit overnight.
- Launder normally in cold water.
- If stain remains stubborn, apply two drops of rubbing alcohol and blot until stain disappears.

Marker

- **Washable marker**: Run hot water over stain as soon as possible, and blot away bleeding marker stains with a clean, dry cloth. Wash normally after stain is no longer visible.

- **Regular marker**: Run cold water over stain as soon as possible, and blot color with a clean, dry cloth. If this does not remove the stain, use rubbing alcohol and blot. Wash after stain is no longer leaving a mark on the blotting cloth.

- **Permanent marker**: This will depend on how long the stain has set. First, add a couple of drops of vinegar to the stained area, and blot with a clean, dry towel. If the stain does not bleed on to the towel, it has already set. Switch to rubbing alcohol to lift the stain with the blotting cloth. Once towel no longer picks up color, run hot water over area to remove the remainder of the ink. If the stain is particularly stubborn, soak overnight, then launder as usual.

Mildew

- Mildew is tough, as it affects the fibers. If you catch it quickly, there is a chance you may still be able to remove it.

- Pour vinegar over the area and hang in direct sunlight.

- If it fades but does not lift completely, add a paste of equal parts of coarse salt and tap water. Lay it flat overnight.

- Rinse the salt with warm water the next day, and repeat the vinegar and sun solution.

Milk

- Run cold water over the stain and blot fabric with a clean, dry cloth.
- If stain is stubborn, soak in cold water overnight.
- Launder in cold water and mild detergent per garment instructions.

Mustard

- Mustard contains a yellow dye known as turmeric. If you use any ammonia-based stain removal product, you will actually set the stain permanently.

- Instead, carefully scrape off excess mustard.

- Run cold water over the stain and blot both sides of the fabric with a clean, dry, light-colored cloth. Repeat this until color no longer appears on the cloth.

- Pour vinegar over the mustard stain and let it set overnight.

- Launder as usual in cold water.

Oil

- Using a clean, dry cloth, blot off excess oil from both sides of the fabric.

- Sprinkle stain with cornstarch to absorb oil, and let it sit for one hour.

- Brush excess cornstarch off and soak garment in basin of warm water mixed with 1 cup of baking soda overnight.

- Launder in warm water and mild detergent the next day.

Paint

- This will depend on the type of paint and how long the stain has set.

- Water-based paint will come out with water and persistent blotting before laundering.

- For oil-based paint stains, first blot dry with a clean, dry light-colored cloth to absorb the stain.

- Repeat process from the other side of the fabric.

- Continue until no more color is coming on to the clean cloth.

- If the stain is not getting lighter, add a drop of olive oil to the area to loosen the stain. Wait for one hour.

- Repeat the cold-water-and-towel-blotting process.

- Pour vinegar on both sides of the stain and let it sit overnight.

- Launder normally in cold water.

- If stain remains stubborn, apply two drops of rubbing alcohol and blot until stain disappears.

Pencil

- First, attempt to erase pencil marks with a standard pencil eraser. This will work on many areas.

- Add a few drops of vinegar to the pencil marks and blot with a clean dry towel.

- Let the vinegar sit on the stain overnight.

- If the stain has not yet vanished, add a drop of clear mild, detergent directly to the stained area before laundering.

- Wash in cold water.

Perfume

- Oils and alcohols in perfume can stain garments, or it may lighten the color of the item.

- For best results, rinse the stained area immediately with warm water.

- Blot with a clean, dry cloth.

- If a mark remains stubborn, carefully apply a couple of drops of vinegar on the area and let it sit overnight.

- Launder in warm water.

- If the fabric is white, diluted hydrogen peroxide may be used in place of the vinegar.

Red wine

- Red wine stains should be treated immediately for best results.

- Pull fabric taut over a sink or basin and pour boiling water over the stain. This should remove the entire stain if you catch it immediately.

- If you cannot treat it immediately, dab the area with club soda to prevent it from setting.

- If the stain has set, use hot water and two towels, blotting the stain out from both sides of the fabric.

- If stain remains stubborn, pour vinegar over the stain and let it sit overnight.

- Launder per garment instructions.

Ring-around-the-collar

- Make a paste of equal parts baking soda and water and apply to stained areas of clothing.

- Press paste into stained fabric and let it sit overnight. This will absorb the oil and deodorize the fabric as well.

- Add ½-cup of baking soda or washing soda to washing machine when laundering.

- If stains remain stubborn, spray area with straight lemon juice and lay flat in direct sunlight, stained area facing up, for two to three hours.

Rust

- Rinse fabric with cold tap water and blot dry with a clean cloth to remove excess rust.

- Once color no longer appears on the cloth, pour lemon juice on both sides of the stain.

- Make a paste from equal parts of coarse salt and tap water, and apply to the top of the stained area.

- Lay flat or hang in direct sunlight for two to three hours.

- Launder normally.

- Rust stains may also be removed by soaking fabric overnight in sour milk.

Scorch marks

- For light scorch marks, rinse fabric with cold tap water and blot dry with a clean cloth to remove mark.

- For a heavier mark, pour lemon juice over affected area and hang in the sun until stain lifts.

Shoe polish

- Using a butter knife, carefully scrape excess residue from stained item.
- Pre-treat with paste made from equal parts of borax and water.
- Rub paste into stained area and let it sit overnight.
- Work through stain again before washing the next day.

Shoe stains on socks

- Soak white socks overnight in warm water and 1 cup of table salt.
- Machine wash in warm water with 1 cup of borax and a clear, mild detergent.

Soy/Worcestershire/steak sauces

- Carefully scrape off excess sauce.

- Run cold water over the stain and blot both sides of the fabric with a clean, dry, light-colored cloth. Repeat this until color no longer appears on the cloth.

- Pour vinegar over the stain and let it sit overnight.

- Launder as usual in cold water.

Sweat

- Make a paste of equal parts baking soda and water, and apply to stained areas of clothing.

- Rub paste into stained fabric and let it sit overnight. This will absorb the oil and deodorize the fabric as well.

- Add ½-cup of baking soda or washing soda to washing machine when laundering.

- If stains remain stubborn, spray area with straight lemon juice and hang in direct sunlight for three hours.

Tea

- Run hot water over area from both sides of fabric and blot with a clean, dry cloth to remove excess color from the tea stain.

- When the cloth no longer catches any color during the blotting process, apply a mixture of baking soda paste made from equal parts of baking soda and water.

- Let the mixture sit on the stain overnight and launder normally in the hottest water appropriate for fabric type.

Tomato sauce

- Carefully scrape off excess tomato sauce.
- Run cold water over the stained area.

- Blot dry with a clean, dry, light-colored cloth to absorb the stain.
- Repeat process from the other side of the fabric.
- Continue until no more color is coming on to the clean cloth.
- Pour vinegar on both sides of the stain and let it sit overnight.
- Launder normally in cold water.

Urine

- Rinse fabric with warm water.
- Pour vinegar on stained area and let it sit overnight. This will attack the stain, as well as deodorize the fabric.

Vomit

- Place affected item in washing machine and fill the machine with cold water. Add 1 cup of table salt and let it soak for one hour.

- Add 1 cup of vinegar to the rinse cycle and launder as usual.

- The salt will prevent stains from setting, and the vinegar acts as a disinfectant and deodorizer.

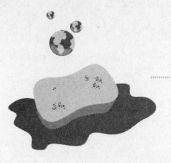

Chapter 16

Taking out the Trash

"Civilization is being poisoned by its own waste products."

— William Ralph Inge, English author

This chapter answers the all-important question of how to dispose of products with dangerous chemicals. Because burgeoning landfills and polluted water are a major concern, there are special requirements for getting rid of things like medications, household cleaners, and leftover paint.

Currently, trash and recycling programs are run on a statewide basis. Additionally, each municipality has its own specific guidelines regarding what you may and may not discard. Most municipalities have designated days and areas for disposing of items such as toxic chemicals, medicines, and other items that are not permissible with routine trash and recycling.

Residential Recycling Programs

Residents obtain recycling containers through their municipality. They each have their own guidelines concerning how items may be discarded and how. For example, you may be permitted to place items in a container at the curb in front of your home. In other areas, you may have to drive the items to a designated unit away from your property. The municipalities make these decisions in combination with the waste retrieval companies. Most companies will accept the following with regular recycling:

- Aluminum food and beverage containers
- Glass (clear, brown, green) food and beverage containers
- Plastic containers with symbols 1 through (and including) 7. The symbols and numbers appear on the bottom of the container. If the item does not have the recycling symbol and a number, it cannot be recycled.
- Empty aerosol cans
- Corrugated cardboard
- Newspapers
- Construction paper, cereal and food boxes, paper towel rolls, or similar
- Printer paper, computer paper, copy paper
- Junk mail
- Magazines and catalogs
- Telephone books

It differs from area to area, but the following are common items that are generally not accepted with routine recycling:

- Paint
- Wax-coated paper
- Materials with food debris
- Plastic bags

- Batteries
- Styrofoam
- Light bulbs
- Mirrors, window glass, ceramics, cookware, bakeware, drinking glasses
- Wood
- Unnumbered plastics
- Coat hangers
- Appliances
- Hazardous or toxic substances

Most areas have special requirements for getting rid of things like medications, household cleaners, and leftover paint. The current trend is to have designated collection days, called "Hazardous Waste Pickup Days," for these types of items so that consumers do not put these items with their regular trash and recyclables.

When replacing your cleaning products, do not just throw the old ones in the trash. If they are too toxic for your home, they will not be good for the drain or the landfill, either. Many communities hold toxics and electronics recycling days and will take these off your hands. Throwing chemicals in the trash or down the drain means they might end up back in your water supply.

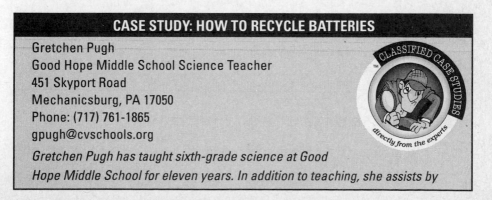

CASE STUDY: HOW TO RECYCLE BATTERIES

Gretchen Pugh
Good Hope Middle School Science Teacher
451 Skyport Road
Mechanicsburg, PA 17050
Phone: (717) 761-1865
gpugh@cvschools.org

Gretchen Pugh has taught sixth-grade science at Good Hope Middle School for eleven years. In addition to teaching, she assists by

CASE STUDY: HOW TO RECYCLE BATTERIES

supervising various clubs and coaching sports. In 2008, she started a club that meant a lot to her personally: "The Good Hope Green Team." The club meets twice a week and works on making a difference in the school and community. They also provide a green tip of the day every day during announcements. One activity the club focuses on is recycling. Using the mantra "reduce, reuse, recycle," they provide drop-off areas in the school for recycling a number of items, such as paper, plastic, aluminum, and batteries.

Throwing batteries in the trash can be harmful to the environment. Over time, chemicals leak out of the batteries and can contaminate our water supply. According to Environment, Health, and Safety Online (EHSO), about 8,000 batteries are discarded annually. They contain heavy metals, such as nickel, mercury, and lead. The corrosion of these batteries can leak acid and lead into the soil and water supply. Many states have regulations in place requiring some form of battery recycling. California mandates recycling for almost all battery types.

Knowing this, I decided to research options for battery recycling here in Pennsylvania. A local environmental club informed me that it is actually acceptable to discard alkaline batteries in the trash. It is not safe, however, to dispose of button batteries, lithium batteries, or any other battery types that are rechargeable. These types of batteries should be taken to places equipped to dispose of these chemicals safely. Electronic stores advertise receptacles for recycling these more harmful batteries.

Here at Good Hope Middle School, we educate the students and staff so they properly dispose of them. Students may bring their harmful batteries into school, and we will recycle them for them if they cannot get to one of the businesses mentioned above. Many people do not realize their harmful effects. Education is the key.

Because regulations and business recycling points differ from area to area, you should check with your specific municipality to determine who takes batteries in your local area. Additional information on batteries is available on the EHSO Web site at **www.ehso.com/ehshome/batteries.php**.

Computers and Other Electronics

Many communities have places that recycle electronics as well. Sometimes a vocational school or local business will set up a location to drop these items off. Often, they are taking these items and using the parts to make new items. Because items like computers become outdated very quickly, this is becoming increasingly common for these items in particular.

Many vendors and recycling organizations do a great job of recovering PCs and monitors for proper disposal, but currently, there is no nationally accepted method for dealing with electronic waste, and the U.S. government chose not to sign the Basel Convention prohibiting the dumping of hazardous waste on developing nations.

Currently, only about 10 percent of computers are recycled. With a lack of regulation, the rest are ending up in landfills. The plastic cases can give off toxic fumes when they are burned. Additionally, other elements of the machines contain heavy metals, such as cadmium, lead, and mercury that can leak harmful chemicals into the groundwater.

Anything with a circuit board can actually be recycled. Many schools and businesses have drop-off locations for these types of items. Check your local area for specifics, but in many cases, the following items may be recyclable:

- Computers, including monitors, keyboards, hard drives, and laptops
- Printers
- Cell phones
- Video recorders
- DVD players
- Digital alarm clocks

Certain electronics companies are starting their own incentive programs to recycle these items.

What About the Data?

It is easy to recover sensitive information from a hard drive; therefore, be sure to take your electronic equipment to a reputable service provider to make sure your data does not fall into the wrong hands. To be safe, it is still a good idea to use a utility that will wipe your hard drive clean of all data.

What About the Trash?

Trash bags are another concern. If you are using plastic trash bags, nothing inside them will biodegrade. But there are some eco-friendly trash bags on the market. They are made from cornstarch-based products, allowing them to biodegrade with the trash. Currently, however, they are more expensive than other trash bags. But things are changing daily; this will probably change as well.

Conclusion

"We must become the change we want to see."

— Mahatma Gandhi

The Real Danger

According to the Centers for Disease Control and Prevention, exposure to toxic chemicals is not a simple, one-time issue. Toxic chemicals accumulate in our bodies over time. This poses a great challenge because cancers and other diseases affecting human organs arise over the course of years or decades, making it difficult to see that it has been years of exposure that led to the problem. These diseases may be, in fact, be the body's response to living with and inhaling toxic chemicals for many years of our lives without realizing the potential dangers.

According to the EPA, approximately 70,000 chemicals are now in commercial production. Many of these are used in household products. Unfortunately, these chemicals can accumulate in the human body through the skin and blood over the years. This can cause cancer and other diseases.

Putting Together a Plan of Action

- Call your municipality to determine your disposal laws.

- Start cleaning out the cupboards — make a plan for disposing of the toxic substances dependent on what you find out from the municipalities.

- For those items you chose to keep, store them in airtight containers. For others, determine how to properly dispose of household cleaning products, paints, solvents, and pesticides. For more information about solid waste management, visit **www.epa.gov/waste/nonhaz/ municipal/index.htm**.

- Buy items like vinegar and baking soda in bulk, and designate bins or jars to store your new, non-toxic cleaning products. Place them in all bathrooms, kitchens, and garage.

- Make a plan to organize, simplify, and start your new, non-toxic cleaning processes.

- Open up the windows and get some fresh air.

Feeling Overwhelmed?

It is time to make some changes. There are many dangerous substances lurking in the average home. You have a lot of money invested in products, and you are not really sure where to start. How can you make some positive changes for your family and the environment without having to gut your home and start over — and without spending a fortune on new products? Do it by taking baby steps. Here is a list of simple, eco-friendly changes you can make around your house without driving yourself or your family crazy. They are so easy that you can start right now — without leaving the house or running to the store.

Simple changes to make today

- Use old rags instead of paper towels.
- Open up the windows.
- Wash your windows and mirrors with vinegar.
- Draw back the curtains and pull up the blinds — sunlight produces solar heat.
- Turn thermostat back 2 degrees in winter and up 2 degrees in summer.
- Unplug appliances when not in use.
- Hang your clothes out (or in) to dry on a clothesline.
- Hang up towels after showering — use multiple times before washing.
- Take your own bags when you go shopping; it eliminates plastic bag waste.
- Only use as much water as necessary.
- Take shorter showers.
- Use food scraps in a compost pile in your garden.
- Take water left in drinking cups or plastic bottles and use it to water the plants.
- Clean as you go: It takes less time, energy, and product.
- Wipe down shower walls while you are still in there. It will be easier to clean.
- Do not pre-rinse dishes going into the dishwasher.
- Do not run the dishwasher unless there is a full load.
- As they burn out, replace light bulbs with fluorescent (CFL) counterparts.

- Wash your clothes in cold water — it is just as efficient.
- Do not run the washing machine unless you have a full load.
- Replace your fabric softener with vinegar in your washing machine rinse cycle.
- Turn off lights, the TV, and other appliances when leaving the room.
- Use crumbled up newspapers for cleaning windows and mirrors.
- Lay old newspapers in your garden to keep weeds under control.
- Place houseplants in your home to improve air quality.

Going green does not mean you have to go nuts. Use common sense regarding the changes you make, and try to think things through before taking action. You are trying to improve conditions for the health of your family and the environment — but do it in a way that makes sense.

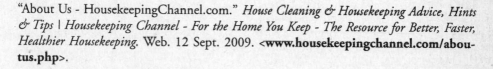

Bibliography

"About Us - HousekeepingChannel.com." *House Cleaning & Housekeeping Advice, Hints & Tips | Housekeeping Channel - For the Home You Keep - The Resource for Better, Faster, Healthier Housekeeping*. Web. 12 Sept. 2009. <**www.housekeepingchannel.com/aboutus.php**>.

Amazon. Web. <**www.amazon.com**>.

American Association of Poison Control Centers. Web. <**www.aapcc.org/DNN**>.

Biernat, Ryszard, and Mariusz Wolosewicz. CDC. Centers for Disease Control. Web. <**http://cdc.gov**>.

Biokleen | Tough on Dirt, Gentle on the Earth. Web. Aug. 2009. <**www.biokleenhome.com**>.

"Castile Soap." Web. <**www.greenlivingtips.com/articles/221/1/Castile-soap.html**>.

Centers for Disease Control. Web. <**http://cdc.gov**>.

"CFL vs. Incandescent: Battle of the Bulb." *Mother Nature Network*. Web. <**www.mnn.com/earth-matters/translating-uncle-sam/stories/cfl-vs-incandescent-battle-of-the-bulb**>.

Consumer Product Safety Commission. Web. <**www.cpsc.gov**>.

"Create Your Own Compost Pile | Composting | US EPA." *U.S. Environmental Protection Agency.* Web. Sept. 2009. <**www.epa.gov/osw/conserve/rrr/composting/by_compost. htm**>.

Dictionary.com. Web. <**www.dictionary.com**>.

Dore, Gustave, and Consolidated Appeals Process. *ToxFAQs.* Centers for Disease Control. Web. <**www.atsdr.cdc.gov/toxfaq.html**>.

EHow | How To Do Just About Everything! | How To Videos & Articles. Web. Aug. 2009. <**www.ehow.com**>.

EKM040. Environmental Protection Agency. Web. <**www.epa.gov**>.

Enviro Media. Web. <**www.greenwashingindex.com**>.

"Environmental Movement History." *EcoTopia.* Web. Aug. 2009. <**www.ecotopia.org/ ehof/timeline.html**>.

Environmental Protection Agency. Web. <**www.epa.gov/dfe/pubs/projects/formulat/ sdsi.htm**>.

"Environmental Quotes." *Grinning Planet.* Web. <**www.grinningplanet.com/environ- mental-quotes/funny-environmental-quotes.htm**>.

"The Farm." *Dickinson College.* Web. Sept. 2009. <**www.dickinson.edu/storg/sisa**>.

Foley, D.O., Mark. "Cleaning Headaches." About.com. Web. <**http://headaches.about. com/od/understandingyourrisk/a/cleaningha.htm**>.

France-Presse, Agence. "Lights out for old 100-watt bulbs in Europe." *Mother Nature Network.* Web. <**www.mnn.com/earth-matters/energy/stories/lights-out-for-old-100- watt-bulbs-in-europe**>.

Green & Healthy Homes | Healthy House Institute - For a Healthier Home - The Resource for a Better, Safer Indoor Environment. Web. Sept. 2009. <**www.healthyhouseinstitute. com**>.

"Green Cleaning Pollution Prevention Calculator." *Office of the Federal Environmental Executive.* Web. Aug. 2009. <**www.ofee.gov/janitor**>.

Green Seal: The Mark of Environmental Responsibility. Green Seal. Web. <**www.greenseal. org**>.

"Health Effects | Mercury | U.S. EPA." *U.S. Environmental Protection Agency.* Web. July 2009. <**www.epa.gov/mercury/effects.htm**>.

"The History of Microfiber." Web. <www.parish-supply.com/treating_disposable_dust_mops.htm>.

House Cleaning & Housekeeping Advice, Hints & Tips | Housekeeping Channel - For the Home You Keep - The Resource for Better, Faster, Healthier Housekeeping. Web. Sept. 2009. <www.housekeepingchannel.com>.

Household Product Database. Ed. Robert M. Wachter, Niraj L. Sehgal, Sumant Ranji, Russ Cucina, and Kaveh G. Schojania. U.S. Department of Health and Human Services. Web. <http://hpd.nlm.nih.gov>.

"Housekeeping Channel Staff Bio - Allen Rathey - HousekeepingChannel.com." *House Cleaning & Housekeeping Advice, Hints & Tips | Housekeeping Channel - For the Home You Keep - The Resource for Better, Faster, Healthier Housekeeping.* Web. Sept. 2009. <www.housekeepingchannel.com/viewbio.php?id=358>.

"Indoor Air Quality." *Volatile Organic Compounds.* Environmental Protection Agency. Web. <www.epa.gov/iaq/voc.html>.

"The Love Canal Tragedy | EPA History | US EPA." *U.S. Environmental Protection Agency.* Web. Aug. 2009. <www.epa.gov/history/topics/lovecanal/01.htm>.

"Mr. Yuk Educational Materials." *Pittsburgh Poison Center.* University of Pittsburgh Medical Center. Web. <www.upmc.com/Services/poisoncenter/Pages/educational-materials.aspx>.

MSDS Online. Web. <www.msds.com>.

National Resources Defense Council. Web. <www.greenpaws.org/products.php>.

Natural Cleaning Products - Nature's Source. Web. Aug. 2009. <www.naturessourcecleaners.com>.

"News - Green Canary Sustainability Consulting." *CPanel®.* Web. Sept. 2009. <http://web03.primusnetworks.com/~greencan/news-item.php?id=160>.

"Polluted Pets: Chemical Exposures and Pets? Health." *Environmental Working Group.* EWG. Web. <www.ewg.org/node/26239>.

Powerful & Natural Cleaning Products & Household Cleaners | Green Works. Web. Aug. 2009. <www.greenworkscleaners.com>.

"Precautionary Principle - The Issues - Sustainable Table." Web. Aug. 2009. <www.sustainabletable.org/issues/precautionary>.

"The Precautionary Principle." *Mindfully.org.* Prepared by The Science and Environmental Health Network Jan2000. Web. Sept. 2009. **<www.mindfully.org/Precaution/ Precautionary-Principle-Common-Sense.htm>**.

"Precautionary Principle." Web. **<www.ienearth.org/docs/pops_precautionary_ted. html>**.

Quotes Daddy. Web. **<www.quotesdaddy.com>**.

Roberts, Edgar V., and Henry E. Jacobs. *www.atsdr.cdc.gov/.* Centers for Disease Control. Web. **<www.atsdr.cdc.gov/toxpro2.html>**.

Rotkin-Ellman, MPH, Miriam, and Gina Solomon, MD, MPH. "Poison on Pets II." (2009). Print. *Safer Detergents Stewardship Initiative.* Designed for the Environment. Web. < **www.epa.gov/dfe/pubs/projects/formulat/sdsi.htm>**.

Seventh Generation. Web. **<www.seventhgeneration.com>**.

Shaklee. Web. Aug. 2009. **<www.shaklee.com>**.

Simple Green. Web. **<www.simplegreen.com>**.

United Nations Environmental Programme. Web. **<www.unep.org>**.

United States. Federal Hazardous Substances act. *Federal Hazardous Substances ACt.* 15 Cong. Cong. Doc. 1261. Print.

Walsh, Bryan. "Eco-Buyer Beware: Green Can Be Deceiving." *Time* 11 Sept. 2008. Print.

"Washing Feather Pillows -- Heloise Hints - *Goodhousekeeping.com.*" - Goodhousekeeping.com. Web. Aug. 2009. **<www.goodhousekeeping.com/home/heloise/laundry/ feather-pillow-washing-jul02>**.

Web. Aug. 2009. **<www.methodhome.com>**.

Web. Aug. 2009. **<www.oxiclean.com>**.

Web. **<www.carbonfootprint.com/calculator.aspx>**.

Whorton, Donald, Ronald Krauss, Sumner Marshall, and Thomas Milby. "Infertility in Male Pesticide Workers." *Www.nap.edu.* The National Academies Press. Web. **<www. nap.edu/openbook.php?record_id=4795&page=585>**.

Wickizer, T. M., and D. Lessler. *Designed for the Environment.* Environmental Protection Agency. Web. **<www.epa.gov/dfe/>**.

Biography

Anne B. Kocsis resides in Camp Hill, Pennsylvania, with her husband of 19 years and three kids. She graduated from Dickinson College in Carlisle, Pennsylvania, in 1987 with bachelor's degrees in English and German. During her senior year in high school, she said she wanted to be a freelance writer and is now living the dream. Her experience includes technical writing, ghostwriting books, writing freelance articles, editing, writing business proposals, and copywriting. During her spare time, she works on a romance novel and enjoys making jewelry, reading, traveling, and going to the beach.

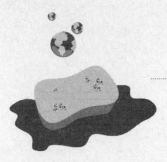

Index

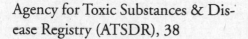